Advance Praise for *Restoring Your Self*
by Peter M. Kalellis

"Never before has a book embraced the age-old quandary of self-acceptance and the development of the true inner peace with such clarity and wisdom. Dr. Peter M. Kalellis extends his experience as a professional with the authorship and warmth of a polished writer and a caring friend. The reader will no longer feel compelled to push aside the normally daunting task of delving into himself or herself, but instead will become motivated and encouraged to welcome transformation through Dr. Kalellis's useful tools and invaluable advice."

—Michelle H. LePoidevin, Editor, Arts & Entertainment
The Westfield Leader and the Times, Scotch Plains-Fanwood, New Jersey

"This is a book that is grounded in the individual's reality yet seeks to awaken the spiritual aspects of human existence. It is a thoughtful, well-organized guide for more effective living. It succeeds in incorporating spirituality into the throes of daily reality."

—Eirum Chaudhri, M.D.

"Take this book into your life, your heart. Dr. Kalellis is a rare treasure. He speaks gently, but with rock-solid insights distilled from a lifetime of training, experience, and prayer. In these pages, he extends his hand and offers to lead you to your Self, at last."

—Wendell Shackelford, Ph.D.

"Dr. Kalellis bridges the disciplines of psychotherapy and spirituality in a book that guides the reader through the emergence of the Self. In essence he supports the Socrates dictum that *the unexamined life is not worth living*. Dr. Kalellis's straightforward presentation is worthy of highest praise."

—Demetria De Lia, Ph.D., Dean of Curriculum
The New Jersey Center of Modern Psychoanalysis

"A must read for those who seek positive change in their lives. Dr. Kalellis's warm and personal style welcomes the reader and encourages self-exploration and personal growth. In every chapter, he offers practical approaches to achieving a happier and more rewarding life."

—Christine McIntyre, MSW, LCSW, Family Therapist

"Following Peter M. Kalellis's bestseller, *Restoring Relationships: Five Things to Try Before You Say Goodbye,* comes a perceptive, provocative, life-altering book that introduces answers for those who are on a quest, seeking what is missing in their lives. *Restoring Your Self* contains five parts; each part consists of four chapters, and each chapter ends with directives that help the reader rediscover the potential of Self and enable the creation of a new and better life. This psycho-spiritual book provides ways of achieving self-evaluation, self-esteem, unconditional self-acceptance, forgiveness, and self-transformation. Read this book and be prepared to cherish the possible and desirable changes in your life."
— *The National Herald,* New York

"Dr. Kalellis knows the human heart. He has great depth of intellect. In *Restoring Your Self* he reaches deep down to the center. His message is luminous and is brimming with new ideas to manage our lives."
— Ernie Anastos, TV News Anchor, CBS 2, New York

"In this insightful and highly practical book, Dr. Peter M. Kalellis carefully guides the reader in the use of strategies for living a happy, more productive life. Dr. Kalellis has the ability to blend psychological insights with specific applications to our daily lives in a warm and inspirational writing style. A highly useful book."
— Frank J. Esposito, Interim President, Kean University

RESTORING YOUR SELF

To my Dear Friend and Colleague, Demetria,

with gratitude & love,

Peter M. Kalellis

May 23, 2002

RESTORING YOUR SELF

Five Ways to a Healthier, Happier, and More Creative Life

PETER M. KALELLIS, Ph.D.

A Crossroad Book
The Crossroad Publishing Company
New York

The Crossroad Publishing Company
481 Eighth Avenue, New York, NY 10001

Printed in the United States of America

Library of Congress Cataloging-in-Publication Data

Kalellis, Peter M.
    Restoring your self : five ways to a healthier, happier, and more creative life / Peter M. Kalellis.
        p.   cm.
    Includes bibliographical references.
    ISBN 0-8245-1934-5 (alk. paper)
    1. Self-actualization (Psychology) – Religious aspects – Christianity. I. Title.
    BV4598.2 .K35 2002
    158.1 – dc21

                                                    2002000683

1   2   3   4   5   6   7   8   9   10   08   07   06   05   04   03   02

CONTENTS

ACKNOWLEDGMENTS

"One nightingale does not betoken spring," says an old proverb, meaning that one person alone cannot accomplish a great task — like writing a book. It is with deep appreciation that I express my thanks to the following persons whose significant contributions have made this book possible.

Patricia A. Kalellis, my wife, provided me with love, emotional support, and sound advice. By creating a nurturing climate at home, Pat made the writing and growth of this book exciting.

The individual personalities of my beloved children, Mercene, Michael, Basil, and Katina, enrich my life and inspire my writing. My daughter Katina, currently a senior at Quinnipiac University, encouraged my progress with unfailing enthusiasm and contemporary information from her studies which she brought to my attention.

Gwendolin Herder, CEO and president of the Crossroad Publishing Company, listened to my ideas and encouraged me to pursue the writing of this book.

Paul McMahon, senior editor at Crossroad, and John Tintera, marketing manager, frequently contacted me and discussed the project. I thank them for their advice.

I am grateful to Margery Hueston and Patti Lawrence for their diligence. Their help has been invaluable in giving shape and form to the manuscript in preparation for the publisher's desk.

John Eagleson patiently read the final draft. His eagle eye made sure that my writing was consistent, clear, and instructive.

Ernie Anastos, CBS-TV news anchor and dear friend, favored me with readings and frequent phone calls, which provided information and inspiration for my writing.

Humbly, I offer this book as comfort and healing for all the survivors who lost their beloved at our nation's tragedy on September 11, 2001. May our Lord God provide healing for their wounded souls.

INTRODUCTION

THIS BOOK IS ABOUT YOU. You probably remember a time when you felt contented, happy, or at peace with your self. You probably wished that those happy days would last for a long time, even for the rest of your life. But something happened, and things did not work out the way you had planned or expected. A promising relationship ended; you lost a good friend or a loved relative; you lost your job; you became ill. You feel upset, stressed out, sad, and directionless. Your self-image has suffered, and you believe that no one can really understand how you feel within.

This book points out ways to restore the true nature of your self, the real human being that you are. Hidden within you is a vast gold mine — goodness, humility, joy, love, peace, spirituality, and talents of every variety — not yet discovered. This may be hard to accept right now, but you do possess an inner God-given treasure. You need only proceed with full confidence to look within your self.

You are not alone! Many of the initiators, instigators, and inventors of our time have lost a sense of mystery about who they are, their purpose, their meaning, their role. Men and women, the originators of all evaluations, judgments, and decisions, the planners of the future are not sure-footed when it comes to attaining perspective on their own selfhood. They often provide ways and means for other people's well-being, but they themselves do not feel fulfilled. They are not happy.

We lack means of comparison necessary for self-knowledge. We know how to distinguish ourselves from other animals physically, but we have no clear picture of who we are. Our ever advancing science and high-tech exposure blanket our world today, saturating and numbing the individual mind. However, as conscious creatures, thinking and reflecting, we can still explore the existence of good and evil among us and bring to light the true understanding of the inner self.

In considering the value and importance of each human being, this book offers five perspectives for healthier and happier days.

Part 1. The Human Dilemma

Part 1 lays the foundation for our theme; we explore and clarify the human dilemma. Four major topics deal with clarity, sensitivity, simplicity, and warmth: (1) Perceptions, (2) What is a human being? (3) What is a woman? (4) What is a man?

Once you begin to understand the essence of your being, woman or man, and have learned to examine your perceptions, then by removing certain major obstacles that stifle your well-being, you will be equipped to move to the next part of your book.

Part 2. Self-Examination

Self-examination helps you to realize who you are; you learn about your self; you learn to express your self; and you discover your true potential. This part of the book explores and helps answer truthfully the important question, Who am I?

Part 3. Self-Evaluation

Part 3 directs your attention to our changing times and the resulting effect on people. Case studies from real life illustrate our attitude toward feelings that do not often change. How do people deal with wounds that are still hurting? Grieving and forgiving provide healing.

Part 4. Self-Acceptance

Part 4 invites you to construct a new definition of self. You define the person you are today. Self-acceptance is the basis and the beginning of self-restoration. In a nonjudgmental way, you will accept your self unconditionally. This enables you to make a smooth transition to where you want to be. You may benefit from the anecdotes of those who encountered troublesome situations and made the transition to a healthier and happier life.

Part 5. Self-Transformation

Part 5 starts with the importance of self-esteem. You transcend the "saturated" self and embrace the sacred reality of the human being. Through the visible self you enter the invisible spiritual part, our soul. Faith and prayer combined help to develop a restored self with a spiritual dimension.

Each chapter of this book concludes with practical directives that I hope the reader finds both informative and inspirational.

PART ONE

THE HUMAN DILEMMA

A human being is God's masterpiece on earth endowed with complex and contradictory attitudes. The way we view ourselves determines, in large part, how we feel about, think of, and react toward the world around us. Humans can love or hate, they can build or destroy, they can be kind or cruel, generous or selfish. They have freedom to make choices.

Chapter 1

PERCEPTIONS

===========

Be aware of your thoughts, and remind your self that the simple
act of thinking — your mental activity — is evidence that there
is an invisible, divine energy that flows through you at all times.
— WAYNE W. DYER

To PERCEIVE IS to become mentally aware of something or someone, of an idea or a notion that makes sense to you. Perception may not necessarily correspond to reality. Perception is an activity of the mind, a process of interpreting what we see, hear, smell, taste, and touch, which enables us to make our existence possible. Through any of our five senses, the mind achieves an understanding of its surroundings.

There are as many perceptions as there are people on this planet. Each person perceives life according to his or her upbringing and cultural and educational background. In addition to the differences between one individual and another, there are also gender differences that distinguish the perceptions of men from those of women. Married couples are forever wrestling with this phenomenon.

Understandably, a woman and a man may look out of the same window at the same scenery and yet perceive it in a different way. One observes the beauty in sky, trees, and flowers and feels inspired, while the other notices how messy the backyard looks and feels disheartened. What they both see is real; it is there. However, their perception and interpretation are different. There is no reason to argue who is right or who is wrong. Neither of them is right or wrong. It is how each chooses to see and perceive reality.

Perception is subjective. It differs from person to person, and it creates either conflict or happiness. Thanks to our minds, we have the capacity to anticipate good and bad situations, to imagine alternative and assorted potential outcomes, and to make plans to try to ensure optimal results.

In the last twenty-five years, we have seen dramatic technological advances. One cannot but admire science's attempt to create smart machines to serve our human needs. However, even the fastest artificial intelligence systems still lack the capacity to create as smooth and as fluid a rendition of reality as the human brain. When these machines are asked to process information in a way that would allow a robot to move purposefully across a room, even the best of them are easily outperformed by a toddler.

It is beyond the scope and purpose of this book to provide an exhaustive anatomical study of the brain and its tireless function to develop perceptions. However, in order to understand our behavior and how we relate to the world, it is important to realize the meaning and power of perceptions, for they dictate our personal fulfillment or lack of it and our daily happiness or unhappiness.

Perceptions combine thoughts, feelings, experiences, and sensations with recognition and judgments. Age plays a significant part in forming perceptions. At the current stage of your life, what looks good to you? What tastes good to you? What kind of music do you like? Does the music you used to like as a younger person appeal to you today? How about your choice of friends? Do you perceive people differently now than you did when you were a teenager? Under your present circumstances — where you are in life — how do you perceive your self as you read these lines?

Perceptions help to interpret and organize our moment-to-moment activities, assigning meaning to the sensations that we receive from our surrounding world. Our perceptions change as we develop, as we experience each stage of our life, as we travel, and as we come in contact with other people. These perceptions follow us every waking moment, designing and directing our lives, affecting or hindering our actions, forming our attitudes about life and living, giving us peace of mind or causing us trouble.

Every day we wake up in the morning in our familiar circumstances, and we return to the same patterns as yesterday. However, if we are not comfortable with these patterns, we can change them by changing our thoughts and actions. Today we can do something different, something creative, imaginative and fresh, pleasant and pleasuring.

Perhaps yesterday you went for a walk. The sun warmed your body and a pleasant breeze caressed your face, giving you a lighthearted feeling. Suddenly, a glum thought over a trivial disappointment that occurred yesterday or a year ago surfaced in your mind and caused a disturbing feeling. As you walked along, you encountered a young couple with a five-year-old boy on a tricycle followed by a playful pup, a golden retriever — your neighbors who live down the block. You said, "Hello," with a smile.

As you strolled around the corner, thinking about your disappointment, you decided to cheer yourself up. The fresh air whetted your appetite and you felt hungry. Less than a quarter of a mile away was a bagel shop. The thought made you smile, and as you picked up half a dozen hot bagels, you hurried home to have breakfast. On the way, you met an elderly couple, friends of your parents, and impulsively you offered to share your bagels with them. You felt happy doing it.

So many things happened on your little outing. Your decision to take a walk provided you with a variety of moods, a variety of feelings, a variety of perceptions.

Today is another day. You are dealing with other things, emotionally you are in a different place, and yesterday's walk seems like a dream. Yesterday's thoughts about the disappointment may have changed. You may even have arrived at a different inference. You are still the same person. Yet when you recount your experience of yesterday, you may notice a variation in your perception. If another person had followed you and observed your interaction with other people or was able to monitor your thoughts, that person would have a different perception from what you personally experienced.

We view our daily encounters through individual experiences — we'll call them "filters." Some filters may be healthy and constructive, while others may be distorted and destructive. But to live effectively, we have to recognize the presence of our filters and make sure that they don't distort our perceptions, causing us to make bad choices.

Rita is a thirty-two-year-old woman whose childhood environment was hostile and violent — an angry mother and an absent father. Raped at the age of five by her grandfather and later by her cousin, as an adult she has a distorted view of relationships, particularly those with men. She perceives men as selfish creatures who take advantage of women. In a period of three years, she was married twice and was twice divorced. Understandably, her painful experiences as a "helpless" child place a filter over her mind that influences the way she perceives people. Hurt by men, she cannot maintain a meaningful relationship with a man. Men are not to be trusted.

Rita may have to modify or even alter her perceptions. She may have to convince herself that all men are not "rats," that there are some good men out there, and one of them could be the right mate for her. She may have to come to terms with the tragedy of her past. She needs to say to her self with conviction, "I was a little girl, unprotected and helpless in the hands of aggressive predators. Now as a capable adult, I can be careful and discreet in my choices."

No longer perceiving herself as a victim but as a survivor of bad circumstances, Rita is able to make a transition in her life.

Resorting to self-pity, feeling sorry for herself, would have provided an escape from responsibility. It would have confused her feelings, blinded her reason, and put her at the mercy of other influences. She decided not to play the role of the tragedy queen we see in old-fashioned dramas. She refused a crown of martyrdom.

Once she acknowledged the fact that her perceptions were particularly influenced by what had happened to her as a child, she was able to choose not to be a prisoner of her past any longer. Nothing could change the reality of her drama, and she didn't have to feel accountable for what had happened. She certainly could not be accountable for having been raped and abused as a child. From the time she reexamined the perceptions of her past, she realized she had to be accountable for the way she would redesign her life.

Rita returned to school. She already had thirty credits in biology from a local college. Some of her credits were recognized, and she was accepted as a second-year student. In her third year, she declared her major to be sociology. During this time, she became very aware of her physical appearance. She lost weight, and every two weeks she made an appointment for a facial treatment and a massage at the Classique Clinic in her hometown. Her dream to have her own cosmetology studio was postponed by marriage.

Rita met Robert, a successful computer programmer, and a year later she married him. Sensitive to her sad past, she treated Robert and their relationship with caution, respect, and dignity. He in turn was cooperative, eager to please Rita, and initiated activities that enriched their marriage. On the day of their third wedding anniversary, Rita and Robert received the greatest gift of their lives, a seven-pound baby girl with blond hair and blue eyes. Her dream of having her own cosmetology studio became a second priority. At least for the present, Rita felt fulfilled in establishing a family. She was happy to put her career on hold.

Human tragedies do not always have a happy ending. David, at thirty-seven, still searching for a rewarding job as a salesman, cannot emerge from the pits of depression. Arguments and quarrels between his parents resulted in a divorce when David was eight. He hated his father for abandoning his family. He grew up with a benevolent couple, his aunt and uncle; his parents were not emotionally available to him. The care and love that his relatives provided was not enough to fill the gap. David missed the security of having his own home with his own parents present. As a teenager, he sought the company of other students whose parents were divorced. Mischief, rape, drugs, and drinking darkened his days for years. He could see no ray of hope in anything. David's perceptions remained fixed: "My world stinks. I have no real family. I'm a loser. I haven't done anything good in my life. Others can be successful. I guess they are smart or lucky. Nobody gives a damn about how I feel. I can't really achieve anything worthwhile."

Do you recognize any part of David's belief system? Do you know anyone who feels this way? Are any of these perceptions yours? Maybe you're holding on to perceptions, beliefs about yourself as being destined for less. Other people are smarter, luckier, for they had better chances in life, but not you. You are the ill-fated one, and it's too bad because you cannot do anything about your situation. Such limited beliefs can only cause you to think of yourself as being less deserving or not being equal to life's challenges.

Maybe this is the time for you to analyze and reconsider your perceptions. Take whatever time you need to thoroughly examine your life, your belief system about your self, your relationships, your past, your job, your future, your friends, God, the world you live in. You have heard the axiom: "An unexamined life is not worth living." This axiom does not refer to life in general, but rather specifically to your life at any given moment.

To examine and redesign your life may be difficult, but it is a necessary task for a healthier and happier direction. As you examine your life, try to invest a lot more time in living. To make the task easier, you can look at your self every day for just a little while. If you postpone the task for too long, it becomes more difficult.

As you start this new direction in your life, restoring your self, it is important that you become aware of your assumptions. Making assumptions implies that you think or perceive something about your self and others and believe that this is reality. In my previous book, *Pick Up Your Couch and Walk*, I used the word "stomatitis" to mean "words come out of our mouth, go directly into our ears, and we believe them to be the truth." We see what we want to see and hear what we want to hear. We don't perceive things the way they are. Instead of making assumptions, it is of personal benefit to seek information and clarification about issues and not jump to conclusions.

We create a chaos of conflicts among ourselves and others by making assumptions. A person who thrives on gossip is also making assumptions, polluting relationships with envy, ill-will, and malice. By defending an assumption, we try to make our selves important or right and prove that somebody else is wrong. What makes us so sure that we are right? Are we omniscient?

A sure way to destroy a relationship is to make continuous assumptions. Often we make the assumption that our loved one should know what we think, how we feel, and what we want. Because our friends or mates know us so well, we assume that they should understand how we think and feel and so do what we want them to do. If they don't respond to us the way we assume they should, we feel hurt and distance our selves.

Barbara, a mature woman in her early forties, fell in love with a man whom she suspected of having an alcohol problem. Bill, five years older than Barbara, charmed her into thinking that he was simply a social drinker. After a couple of embarrassing lapses, she confronted him about his drinking. His response was, "There is nothing to worry about. It won't happen again." She believed him, and assuming that the genuine love she felt would change him, she married him.

Did Bill change? Hardly six months went by, and he returned to his drinking, lying to himself and to his wife that he could control himself. Barbara's loving concern did not change anything. Before their first wedding anniversary, angry at Bill and at herself for assuming that he would change, she filed for divorce.

Any relationship will improve immensely when we do not make assumptions. Conflicts and quarrels will be eliminated when we communicate clearly, honestly, and directly. If something seems obscure and you don't understand it, have the courage to ask questions. We don't need to make assumptions when we get an answer.

As you become aware that perceptions are subjective and, therefore, personal and you accept them as your own mental activity, you don't need to defend yourself or prove that you are right. Your life will be easier when you say boldly: "This is how I see things, and it's okay if you see things differently." Eventually, the habit of making assumptions will diminish, conflicting opinions will not be threatening, and your interaction with other people will be rewarding.

For Your Consideration

~ Think of your capacity to check the accuracy of your perceptions. How you perceive your self as you enter the arena of life and try to make a sensible living is significant for your happiness or unhappiness.

~ It will be to your advantage to avoid unnecessary assumptions about who you are and develop a more positive perception of your self. Having respect for your self implies, at least, that you will choose not to do harmful things to your self.

~ Other people's perceptions and assumptions about you — those of parents, teachers, peers, relatives, mass media — are not always accurate. Develop your perception of your self to describe your self adequately.

~ As you process your perceptions, choose the good parts of your personality and use them. Do not choose to act on your assumptions, although some assumptions could become motivating fantasies in your life — which can be tested.

~ The way you perceive and accept your good qualities and your limitations can be a positive turn in your life. Test your perceptions instead of using grandiose assumptions.

If you cannot sing, do not pursue the idea of becoming an opera star. If the stage is important to you, study theater or learn how to dance!

Chapter 2

WHAT IS A HUMAN BEING?

It would be so wonderful to feel good about ourselves again, to be able to rise above the voices of nagging parents, teachers, and other ghosts from our growing-up years and feel we are people to be loved and admired. — HAROLD S. KUSHNER

CONTEMPLATING THE IMMENSE distance we have covered scientifically and technologically and the mysterious unknown that looms before us, we can ask ourselves, What does it all mean? What are we on this planet? As we experience life, its successes and failures, moments of triumph and exaltation as well as its times of despair and disillusionment, we narrow the focus on ourselves, and we ask, Who Am I?

Every time we raise this question, we are confronted by a multifaceted mystery. Asking, What is a human being? is similar to asking, What is God? Both are universal and difficult questions. Since the beginning of time, prophets, philosophers, teachers, and sages have wrestled with these questions, and throughout the ages they have presented the world with answers, however limited.

The Greeks, who initiated logic, were rather pessimistic about humans. A strain of dualism in early Greek philosophy interpreted spirit and matter as distinct elements in a human being: the spirit was thought as essentially good, whereas matter was essentially evil. Therefore, the body was the seat of all evil in human beings.

Plato, a staunch proponent of dualism, one day described a human as a two-legged animal without feathers. Later that day, Diogenes brought to the marketplace a rooster despoiled of its feathers and announced solemnly, "Behold, the man of Plato!" It was more than a crude joke. It was a declaration that all definitions of a human are ultimately inadequate.

While pondering the mystery of the human being, we can consider some biblical perspectives. We read in the Bible:

21

I look up at Your heavens, made by Your fingers, at the moon and stars You set in place — ah, what is man that You should spare a thought for him, the son of man that You should care for him? Yet You have made him little less than a god, little more than an angel. You have crowned him with glory and splendor. (Ps. 8:3–5)

The biblical story of the Creation allows us to realize the high esteem that God has for His sovereign creatures. After the disobedience of Adam and Eve, although God expelled them from Paradise, He bestowed upon them the greatest blessing, unconditional freedom. The first man and woman were then able to make their own history, develop their latent powers, achieve a new harmony with nature as fully developed individuals going beyond that former condition of harmony in which they were not wholly free.

This is evidence of God's ultimate expression of love for us, affording us the freedom to use our attributes, our powers of reason, and our natural skills to fashion our lives to the full extent of our capacities.

God does not interfere with our choices. He may sustain and instruct and guide us through His messengers, the prophets and sages, who keep clear the vision of the human race. Essentially, we are left alone to reconcile that dualism in our nature, to harmonize the warring elements of good and evil that coexist within each of us. God may be disappointed in some of the things we do, but He is never disappointed with who we are: fallible people struggling with the knowledge of good and evil.

Christian theology provides a plan of salvation for all people. God intervenes in human history: in a supreme act of love God sends His own Son to redeem and restore humankind. His only Son defeated the devil and destroyed death with His own death. As a result, evil cannot control our lives unless we allow it. We can overcome evil by doing good. Evil forces can be considered as ever present realities, yet a human being, by the grace of God, can be free from these by making good choices.

The definition of God by humans remains incomplete, in spite of the efforts of the most advanced minds. Inspired theologians and biblical scholars continue to make eloquent interpretations of the attributes of God. We leave the definition of God and His presence in our life to reverent hearts and minds. But for our purposes, it might be of benefit to explore the question: "What constitutes a human being?"

We have all heard of "the whole person" or "the well-rounded individual." These popular terms evoke only the pleasant prospect of graciously enlarging the self. Some people take extension courses, study texts, develop constructive hobbies, explore different modalities of therapy, or take an active part in a social movement. Actually, the whole person is not whole without such unpleasant realities as anxiety, despair, fear, guilt, illness, death. The way we deal with these inescapable unpleasant realities without having them overtake our psyches is a matter of individual choice.

Touch, feel, move, experience your self. You have a body that consists of flesh, bones, muscles, and blood — your physical self, made up of many elements. These elements are systematically organized to provide physical growth and maturity by an inner power beyond your control. This is rather staggering. I feel awe and offer gratitude for this miracle of life — our growth from conception through childhood and adulthood in spite of trials and tribulations. Is it by chance? Or is it by divine providence?

A part of us is spiritual, a mysterious element, great, eternal, and infinite. In embracing this concept, we must adjust our way of thinking and behaving. This is our challenge if we truly wish an authentic understanding of our human nature.

We are endowed with minds that think, plan, and organize our lives and environments to meet our needs. God guides our steps for the benefit of our personal needs.

As a baby, without your permission, you were committed to the world and to the life that lay ahead. When the umbilical cord was cut and tied, that was the awesome moment when, tiny and helpless, you needed total care of a mother or mothering figure to survive. Despite its human shortcomings, your family formed supportive ways to protect you from the larger society and prepare you to merge with it.

As an adolescent, partially free from parental control, you sought ways to relate to others who were also seeking ways to connect and to adjust to the larger family, society. During these youthful years, an inner force kept you going. You probably felt like Archimedes, who said, "Give me a place on which to stand and I can move the earth." You felt powerful enough to face any obstacle. Perhaps in an effort to find a place or a secure way of life, you embraced a cause or a lifestyle that provided standards for judging what was right or wrong, what was pertinent or irrelevant.

When you began to sense the need for a job, the turbulent teenage years found some direction. Maybe at that time you made a decision about a career. As you thought of choices, problems were either repressed or settled, for your attention and energy were needed to prepare yourself for the future. What you decided to do during those early years most likely helped you to answer the query, Who am I?

At this juncture, it mattered little what you decided to do; what truly mattered was your commitment and effort to make whatever you chose to do interesting and rewarding. You sought outward to find a way of life that would satisfy your physical needs. You wanted to be happy. At the same time, you turned inward seeking resources, weighing liabilities for your emotional needs, and possibly asking questions: "What are my strengths, my talents? What are my deeper desires that need fulfillment?" You probably sought inner joy and personal contentment.

As a young adult at the height of your physical and mental vigor, you launched yourself into your future, and your energies and talents were tested. Growth and development became priorities. Your independence from your parental family motivated you to achieve interdependence with others and a connection with a place in society. Usually, vocational choice precipitates marital choice, two key decisions for your life.

Regardless of how you prepared to enter adult life, you had to realize that you could not invest any more time and effort to find solutions to old problems. Simply, you could not remake your past. Nobody can. You accepted — or repressed — your past while hoping to improve your present and your future. Your choices of an occupation and of a mate were decisions resulting from the influences that you had internalized during growing years. While both of these choices are often made as a rather natural progression, they are both results of the total developmental process together with realistic opportunities.

To sum up, all human beings go through a similar process, making transitions from one stage of life to another to preserve a sense of *self* — an intactness and wholeness of self — distinct from society. The process of growth may have variations in different cultures or societies, yet failure to become a distinct individual in any society leads to conformity or, worse, loss of self. When societal ways run counter to a person's concept of self, the individual feels disillusioned and in danger of alienation. Erik H. Erikson put it rather poignantly: "In the social jungle of human existence there is no feeling of being alive without a sense of identity."

At this point, common sense reassures us that we do have a self of our own, an identity in a process of change. Whether you like your self or not is not the point. What matters is that you are alive, you have a place in society, and currently you are reading this book. In your reasoning abilities, you are different from other people. You have needs similar to those of some people, or goals similar to those of others, but in reality, you are different. There is a place for you in this world, and your task is to make that place better for your self and others who share it.

Regardless of what your life is like, whatever the truth about you is, avoid labeling yourself with these popular characterizations:

Addict	Histrionic
Antisocial	Hysterical
Anxious	Narcissistic
Authoritarian	Neurotic
Bi-polar	Obsessive-compulsive
Bulimic	Paranoid
Burned-out	Psychopath
Controlling	Repressed
Depressed	Schizophrenic

These are all terms of mental deficit which have gradually entered our vocabulary. They discredit the individual and draw attention to problems, incapacities, or shortcomings.

As psychiatrists, psychologists, and psychotherapists try to explain undesirable behaviors or disturbing symptoms, they generate a technical vocabulary of deficit, and the *Diagnostic Manual* increases in size every year. The language is slowly disseminated to the public at large so that the average person, too, can become conscious of mental health issues. As people acquire the vocabulary, they also come to suspect and to see self and others in these terms. They diagnose themselves, engendering further perceptions of illness and often seek the professional as essential for cure. Others believe so strongly in the promises of drug advertisements that they tell their doctor what to prescribe. Personally, I maintain that nobody and no medication can cure anybody. A professional — sometimes with the proper medicine, at other times without — can facilitate the healing process, and that is all. The cure already exists within each person. Get deeper into your self and learn from your self what you must do. You have choices.

For Your Consideration

~ Through discovery of what a human being is, you will encourage your self to see who in the world you are. And knowing your self and appreciating your unique gifts and abilities, you will make choices that will help you to find a rewarding direction in life.

~ Regardless of who you are and how you have evolved through your life as a human being, when you make careful and solid choices from this moment on, you will experience a newness of life. You will feel an inner joy, because your genuine self will begin to emerge.

~ Regardless of what people might think of you, simply be yourself, be the person you really are. As you demonstrate honor and respect for your self, make your own decisions about what you think is best for you, ever mindful that you live in a world of people who have their own needs and are in quest of their own happiness.

~ Avoid competing and comparing your self with others. Competition does not create character; it exposes it. It is wasted time and energy. Combat the tendency to look at others to evaluate your self. You are not them. The only thing that counts is how you use the potential you possess to achieve your strongest sense of self.

~ All humans exist in two states of life, the physical and the spiritual. We are both what we are and what we might become. Treat your physical part with care and respect. Nurture your spiritual part, your soul, by acknowledging its existence and loving it.

Chapter 3

WHAT IS A WOMAN?

═══════════════

"What is that mystery?" Zorba asks. "What is a woman, and why does she turn our heads? Just tell me, I ask you, what is the meaning of that?" He interrogates himself with the same amazement when he sees a man, a tree in blossom, a glass of cold water.
— NIKOS KAZANTZAKIS

HOW CAN ANY man know what a woman is? She is God's masterpiece. A woman is a human being very much like a man and yet significantly different. A woman's life is quite different from a man's, and quite different from one part of her own life to another. Like the male child, the female child's identity is initially formed and shaped by her family of origin. Later, school, peers, society, and personal experiences enhance her identity.

In an effort to help you restore your self, let's highlight how your identity came to be. Your parents or parental adults had a great impact on your life. The unique person that you are has its roots in your family background. If you have siblings, you may notice similarities with them, but ultimately you realize that you are also a different person. As you are aware, every family has its own belief system and lifestyle, which strongly impacts the development of children.

For example, if you came from an "enmeshed family," you had to obey without recourse the commands, "Do as I say." "Don't feel as you do — feel the way I say you should." Actually you had no choice. You were lumped together with other members of your family in such a way that your individual identity was difficult to develop. You probably suffered emotionally, but you were not able to express your feelings. It did not matter to other members of your family what you thought or how you felt. You had to conform to the undefined rules of conformity and control that permeated your home environment.

If you grew up in a "disengaged" family, you probably experienced a lot of confusion, and as you developed, you had no guidance. Each member was distant from the other, followed his or her own undefined direction, and did not care how you felt. As a result, you may have developed some dysfunctional or even destructive patterns of relating with other people, and you may still feel insecure.

However, if you were fortunate enough to grow up in an "engaged" family, you have developed a more balanced lifestyle. You were able to distinguish between conformity and irresponsible behavior. You understood what respect meant for each member of the family. In your interaction with each other, you learned to respect boundaries. Even though there were conflicts and disagreements, your family unit was able to provide solutions. In the interim, you had a sense of security, self-worth, and trust. If your needs were not met and you felt angry, in time you learned how to cope, how to address angry feelings, how to forgive, and how to love.

Regardless of which of the above family systems you were raised in, each of your parents or whoever was in charge of your developmental years contributed toward your identity. You observed and adapted aspects of their personalities, healthy or unhealthy, and made them your own. Some of these might still be present in your life. You also had received from God a blueprint of your own growth within the core of your self. Now as a mature adult you have a choice of keeping and amplifying those good qualities that you inherited growing up and of discarding whatever is no longer of value to you.

You emerged into the larger family — neighborhood, school, society — and as a young girl you behaved differently from young boys. Because good behavior was socially acceptable, you had less need for internal self-approval. Motivation and self-reliance were not an issue with you, since you had learned that good behavior was rewarded.

Conceivably, during your puberty years you received a double message, perhaps an ambiguous message, about your body and sex. One message was that it was desirable to have someone love and marry you: you had won someone's attention and approval. It was desirable to be able to menstruate and, in proper time, to have babies: you had entered the world of adult women. The other message was that menstruating was uncomfortable, inconvenient, and unclean; having babies was confining, risky, and monumentally painful. Inevitably, these two messages had a direct link to your inner world.

Psychologist J. Bardwick states: "Girls are not significantly stressed nor pressured until puberty, and there is a critical delay in the establishment of an independent concept of the self and internalized criteria of self-esteem."

In the context of school, you continued to enjoy the rewards of good behavior; approval came your way as you excelled in academic tasks as well. Of course you were encouraged to achieve academically, and also athletically, to compete with the male. Suddenly, in adolescence, the rules were changed. You were expected to change your goals of individual achievement and concentrate on attracting, not outdistancing, the male. Having internalized certain values of success, you discovered that masculine values no longer applied to you; yours were to secure a job or a career, to find a mate, get married, and rear a family. Whether married or single, you still felt equally important in society to men. Granted, it was never put in quite such blatant terms, but the dynamic was nonetheless there.

Either by choice or circumstances, some women prefer to live a single life. They seem to enjoy their freedom and independence. One of my clients, after her first marriage failed, decided to return to school and pursue a career as a physiotherapist. She found this work very fulfilling and decided to dedicate herself to helping her patients. Parallel to her work, she appropriated time to build a home. In her words, "My home and garden are my earthly paradise. It took effort, money, and time to build this home of my dreams. Now I truly enjoy each hour I spend in it. After I have taken good care of the pains and aches of my patients, I return to my haven, my own home, where I find peace and contentment. My home and garden are major contributors to my wellness and happiness. It is my sanctuary which I appreciate, decorate, and maintain with care and sensitivity. It is where I surrender, rest, and replenish my strength." This was her choice.

Most women prefer love and marriage. The day a woman enjoys her first love, it cuts her in two; in addition to how she has developed to be, regardless of how independent and self-reliant she has been, she becomes another woman on that day. Now she has found the man of her heart, the one in whose presence she experiences joy, security, and love. Her emotional apparatus reaches peak moments. She becomes a visionary, planning a life with her beloved, making him happy, giving and receiving love, and creating a nest where her potential family will find fulfillment.

When a career woman decides to get married, she makes a major transition in her life. She replaces the stage where she provides performance and receives the rewards of a paycheck and possible prestige with the home front and its domestic responsibilities. Not that man should be exempt from domestic responsibilities. However, when the childbearing, birthing, and caring begin, it is the woman who usually carries the heavier load. The Mr. Mom myth in rare cases proves effective; it does contribute a little support to lighten the burden, but essentially the woman tends to provide most of the emotional and family nurture, even if she has to work outside her home.

In our times, regardless of what the preferences are in terms of staying home and taking care of the children in the preschool years, the escalating expenses of living compel the woman to join the workforce. As much as she likes to nurture her neonate, in some cases a woman may have to work outside the house within two to four weeks after she gives birth. Many well-intentioned families can hardly meet expenses even if both parents work. This is their reality. Consequently, the woman feels responsible, enters the workplace, and brings home her earnings. In many cases the wife makes more money than the husband, and men look at that possibility with an envious eye. Should they play the game "I make more than you do," the marriage can go off balance. But in a mature and loving relationship it does not really matter as long as they both contribute.

As a mother, the woman is another person than she was without a child. She carries the fruit in her womb for nine months. Something pleasant and at times uncomfortable grows into her life that never again departs from it. She is a mother. After midnight when parents and children are sound asleep, dead silence permeates the household. Suddenly, from one of the rooms comes a whimper that only the mother hears. She rushes to the baby's room. Red in the face, with tears streaming down her cheeks, the little girl is now screaming at the top of her lungs. The mother picks her up, holds her under her chin, and the screaming stops. In the mother's arms the baby senses security. Peace!

To describe perceptions of maternal relationships would require another book. Our purpose here is to offer a concept of what a woman is in our times. Women's lives, roles, and behaviors have changed greatly over the past forty years. They are more stressful in many ways. Because a woman lacks training and experience in the exercise of power equal to that of men, she may feel awkward or guilty exploring a role of her own with a decisive and assertive self rather than a reactive one.

When a woman behaves according to expectations of others with little regard for her own needs or desires — and women do behave in this way to maintain harmony — the result is stressful. Women are justified in protesting and rising up against long-standing prejudicial attitudes promoted by a male-oriented society. In the protest, however, the woman can lose perspective if she allows her emotions to take over without a strong dose of logic. The outcome may be destructive.

Consider Susanne's situation. She was a thirty-eight-year-old working woman and wife. She felt able to work and to think well as long as she worked on her ideas and plans in her own house. However, she felt she could not bring her ideas into the work setting. In her own words, "I wish I could bring my inside self outside." Susanne sensed that she could not get her own perceptions, evaluations, and judgments across to her employer, although she had important contributions to make. Had she dared to speak her mind, she would disrupt the whole work scene. In other words, she would be characterized as a disturbing element — and that was not the way she felt she should operate. She did not want to give the impression that she was a destructively aggressive person.

For some women it is more comfortable to repress personal feelings than it is to speak up. Terrible as that can be, it is still better than to feel powerful, if power makes for destruction. However, whatever power women may possess, they tend to use it for the benefit of others, enhancing the position, capabilities, and effectiveness of other people while simultaneously increasing their own power. In some way, this feeling reinforces their tendency to be caretakers, nurturers, or even rescuers.

This tendency has its own inherent danger when a woman with all good intentions tries to rescue a loser. She loves him, and that's what counts. The tragedy is that these naive young or older women find derelicts and fall in love with them although they know their bad and abusive habits. Often a woman's fantasy is that she will reform her chosen one, and gradually he will be a good mate. In my practice, a week does not go by without my having to deal with such a case. Most of the time, women who try to rescue losers end up with broken hearts or broken lives.

My experience indicates that women are more likely to be victimized in their effort to save "the lost sheep" than are men. With some understanding of their motivation and deep empathy for their pain, I suggest that they pull back and analyze the results of their efforts. If their choice of a man proves to be a mistake, I ask the brokenhearted woman to forgive her self, to release her self from the tyranny of self-recrimination. Mistakes can be the best lessons and last a lifetime.

In and outside of my profession, I stand in awe and admiration as I experience the enormous emotional apparatus and power with which women are endowed. By taking charge of this power and using it constructively, a woman can be very effective in whatever endeavor she undertakes.

What we need as a well-informed society is an honoring and valuing of the feminine principle. Masculine roles are neither more important nor less important than feminine roles; both are needed and are of equal value. They are, however, different. In ways that are unique to her sex, a woman's psychic behavior is inextricably bound to her physiology. It has to do with the female reproductive processes and a highly complex endocrine system. Since a woman's life goals are often closely linked to her body, the dynamics of self-esteem and self-concept are likely to be quite different from those that operate in a man.

It is not biology alone that affects female behavior. Familial, societal, and cultural factors have their own influences and generate their own difficulties. For the most part, and for reasons largely undefinable to them, women have, until very recent times, assumed the role of silent sufferer. Recently, however, more and more women have been finding their voices and have been able to articulate forcefully both the nature and the causes of their dissatisfaction.

Twenty years after *The Feminine Mystique* hit the shelves, Betty Friedan wrote a new introduction to the book. In it, she marveled at women's advances since 1963: "Firewomen, chairpersons...takeout food...women judges, rabbis, pastors, priests, women prime ministers...women's studies...more women now going to college than men...the two-paycheck family....Who could have predicted some of these? Not I, certainly."

Perhaps Friedan could not have predicted the changes, but she played her part in helping to bring them about. She participated in forming the National Organization for Women (NOW). One of NOW's goals was to persuade Congress and the states to adopt the Equal Rights Amendment.

Since that new beginning, the general structure of society has changed, and many women have reached the top of the ladder. They anchor news programs, report the news, and make the news as members of Congress, the Senate, the Cabinet, the Supreme Court, and as elected and appointed officials in the nation's federal, state, and city councils. Women are appearing, in increasing numbers, in scientific and technological fields, sports, military, religion, politics, business. In many of these areas, women are carving out successful careers today.

Inner conflicts arise between the traditional concept of motherhood and the newer concepts of success and achievement. Ambivalent loyalties emerge. Is she being a "good mother" or a "selfish mother" if she achieves professional success? We are accustomed to the idealized notion of motherhood as a "divine attribute," to the classic "All I am I owe to my mother." Even a modern woman has qualms about striking out from the nest, even though it be empty of dependent young. These doubts compound the self-doubt to which a woman is susceptible in struggling with her self-image.

While a husband is progressing confidently in his career and is making new demands on his wife to be a vibrant companion, she is facing issues of power struggle. She is feeling "narrowed and impatient, although probably ill-equipped to be something more." She knows she must venture "out there" and succeed at something so that she can develop the self-image and self-pride she must acquire if she is to live out the rest of her life with any sense of fulfillment. This is a time when a woman must begin to build the independence so long denied her. She must take risks, and risks always require courage. Sometimes in her effort to gain recognition as an equal partner either in marriage or in an intimate relationship, the woman falls into the trap of competing with her mate. "If he can do it, I can do it also. Whatever he does, I can do it better," she may think, and engage in a power play that leaves her restless. Competition fueled by tinges of jealousy breeds fear, and fear breeds comparisons and more competition, which result in endless quarrels and in an unbalanced existence. A self-reliant woman feels no desire to compete or otherwise prove herself, to herself, to her mate, or to anyone else. She develops her God-given talents and uses them wisely for her own emotional growth and for the benefit of her intimate others. A woman who has developed a good self-image and continues to nurture it by employing her inner resources does not have to be jealous or competitive. She has already accepted unconditionally who she is, and she feels in harmony with her self and her surroundings. Of course these principles are equally true for men. But in this chapter the focus is on the woman.

The more we explore the concept of self, the firmer our convictions become about the differences between individuals of high and low self-esteem. A woman with a good self-image is more independent, creative, and confident in her judgment and ideals, more courageous and socially liberated — that is, self-determining — more psychologically stable, less anxious, and more success-oriented than a woman with a poor self-image. On the whole, she is happier and more effective in everyday life.

Women at the low end of the self-esteem scale tend to show a lack of trust in themselves. They are reluctant to express themselves in a group, especially if their ideas are likely to be seen as novel. They would rather listen than participate. Self-conscious and *closed*, they are less successful in interpersonal relationships. As a result, they are likely to be less active in social, civic, and political affairs because they feel inadequate and insecure.

Having explored some of the reasons for women's feelings of low self-worth, we must acknowledge that nature and society have conspired to deal the woman a stacked deck. Cultural and physiological *norms* often place her at a disadvantage. As the societal handicap is removed and the biological one understood, we will see women successfully resolving their role conflicts, confronting moral issues, realizing themselves more fully, and, with their great natural strength and resiliency, demolishing the shibboleth of "the weaker sex."

Women have been wrestling with issues of justice, responding to conflicts with confidence, and pursuing viable solutions. When confronted with controversial questions — such as abortion or cloning — they respond according to their personal convictions. Generally speaking, a woman believes her main principle is not to hurt others and not to go against her own conscience. Above all, she must remain true to her self. When she faces a moral dilemma and cannot decide which direction to take, she does not hesitate to seek professional help or spiritual guidance.

Today, for every woman there is a personal journey toward the development of all her emotional, mental, intellectual, and spiritual faculties. We can hear her voice whispering gently: "I am a human being. I must no longer be defined by roles. I believe in the primacy of the human being not conditioned by gender. My life on this planet has a purpose that I need to pursue." Could there be a more practical and beautiful message?

If your self is defined by others, you will probably have a hard time accepting it. If your personal evaluation is based on comparisons, you may feel worthy or worthless or lukewarm. When you compare yourself with others, you are entering an endless and unjust warfare. You are who you are, and conceivably you can accept and convert your qualities into creativity. However, if you compare yourself with the camera-ready models or movie stars and set their level of appearances and success as your guide, you may end up feeling disappointed. These selected few are not really appropriate models for comparison. A woman reading a magazine or watching television might compare herself to a celebrity more often than a man does. Commercial advertisements appearing in mass media are cleverly designed to convince consumers that the product will make them more beautiful or younger or even bring happiness into their lives. How real is that?

Of course we may admire celebrities, talk about them, and have fantasies. When we catch ourselves imitating and trying to be like one of them or like anyone else, then our own self suffers. Rather than enjoying and developing our own qualities, we are wasting psychic energy emulating someone else whom we cannot be.

The theme of this book is *restoration of self*. Although praise from others gives each of us a lift, the strength of your self-importance is within you, provided you are willing to look for it. You are not worthless or helpless. You are you, regardless of how shy or down you are on your self. You are able to read this book; you can go over this chapter once again and reassess aspects that hold a meaning for you; the contents may generate new and useful ideas. You are capable of making decisions; you are able to render help where help is needed. Help your self to become who you want to be.

Why not allow your self to be in touch with your total personality, both positive and negative qualities? Remember, imperfection is part of our human condition; we can try to change what can be changed realistically. Inner growth is possible provided that is what you want. If your inner self is tarnished or fragmented, *it can be restored*. Start by accepting your self unconditionally.

If you truly want to restore your self, no obstacle or excuse can hold you back. You may have learned from parents, teachers, peers, and mass media that you are incomplete, inadequate, and therefore dependent. However, must you use your inadequacies as defenses and remain idle? Surely not. If your perception of self is low, the world is more predictable because you do not have confidence to do anything new about your situation. The status quo promises security. If you do not try something new or different, you will not fail. Fear of failure prevents you from taking an active part in life. Is that what you would like to be — passive?

For Your Consideration

~ Think of yourself not as a woman but as a human being with strengths and weaknesses; you are a person. Evaluate your strengths and make a plan to use them constructively. Keep your negative qualities at bay until you are able to deal with them in a nondestructive way.

~ In whatever stage of your womanhood this book finds you, enjoy that state. Think of your life as a long voyage with many ports on the way. Cherish each stop and take hold of whatever it offers — activities, experiences, fun.

~ Past memories, especially the ugly ones, are like bad tenants: they are taking up space and not contributing one cent! Replace them with plans for today and remind your self that the past cannot change; the present and the future certainly can.

~ Should you find your self in any relationship that causes pressure, explore the possibility that you might be in a *power struggle*. If you discover that the interaction is competitive and that you must win, inadequacy may be the problem.

~ Come into creative contact with others who are enthusiastic about life and establish a relationship that is positive. Think of what you are able to offer. Even if it is a small contribution, do something for those who need help. Do something that gives you inner joy for doing it.

Chapter 4

WHAT IS A MAN?

===

*Every man has to seek in his own way to make his own self
more noble and to realize his own true worth.*
— ALBERT SCHWEITZER

EACH ONE OF US is a human being before being a man or a woman.
You and I, man or woman, have roles and functions to fulfill, indi-
vidually and socially. As you read this chapter, you may notice that
some of the male characteristics are easily translatable to women.

Men may or may not accept traditional male roles. Men are free
to choose to get married or not, to accept the role of husband or of
father. It is the man's choice to refuse to be identified as the defender,
the fighter, the provider, and so forth. A man is a living being with all
the dignity and potential of a whole human being. Men have the right
to expect respect from women and parity with them, just as women
have the right to expect respect from men and parity with them.

In our times, some men are making genuine efforts to liberate
themselves from their emotional straitjackets, from labels attained
or assigned. Men, more than ever before, want to be warmer, more
loving, and affectionate; that is, they are becoming more conscious
of their feminine side or self. Women cherish a gentle, romantic,
and expressive attitude from their men. They admire assertiveness,
emotional involvement, and honesty in their men.

Some men have a hard time defining who they are. Instead of
accepting and applying their human qualities and characteristics as
males, they conform to the majority or they settle for stereotypes.
Take, for example, the husband whose wife earns a much larger
salary than he does. She is excited about her contribution to their
household. Instead of being happy, the husband is upset because of
his perception that men should be bringing home more money than
their wives. Not wanting to reveal the reason for his discontent, he

finds fault with her job and criticizes her. As a result, the marriage goes off balance.

Many men cannot express feelings. Does that mean they are less than human? All human beings have feelings and need to clarify, develop, and work with them. I have seen men crying, laughing, and displaying other deep feelings when appropriate. A man who withholds his feelings reveals his inability to deal with them. Yet some men believe it is not *manly* to be emotional. Many pretend they are not affected by strong emotions. If a man ignores or represses his feelings, however, he inadvertently pushes them into his subconscious. When the tank of the subconscious overflows, then men are controlled or victimized by their feelings. A man who denies the existence of his feelings may become depressed, or he may escape into a world of fantasy.

After seven years of what his wife called "a good marriage," Ted decided to move out of the house. His reason? Too much stress both at work and at home. He was afraid he might have a heart attack. He confided to his friend Phil that he was dissatisfied with his marriage. He could no longer talk to his wife. She had been asking him too many "Whys": Why don't you talk to your boss? Why don't you look for another job? If you are depressed, why don't you see a therapist?

When Phil asked him if he ever talked to his wife about his real feelings, he answered, "I don't think she would ever understand how I feel." Drawing such a definitive conclusion and not confronting what really bothered him — lack of energy, aging, feeling unaccomplished — Ted sought an escape. So he moved into an apartment and felt better being alone, at least for a while. He thought that he was entitled to a sort of spontaneous and unaccountable life, wining and dining with his friends, going to parties, and traveling.

At times, intellectualization is a strong defense mechanism that engages men in a power play. Men learn early to compete and surpass others. Think of your self. Since boyhood you have been programmed to value your self in terms of strength, achievements, successes, and victories. As an adult, having finished school and having ventured forth to meet the *real* world, you discovered other achievers — successful and victorious adults. While you climbed upward or moved along among peers and colleagues, inner insecurity and doubt often could be pacified only by rationalization.

Mark's experience serves as an example. When Mark was twenty-six, a headhunter placed him with a very aggressive financial firm, which paid him well. Besides a handsome salary, his commission increased month by month, giving him a six-digit income he could hardly believe. However, by the end of the year, his initial enthusiasm faded into a nagging dissatisfaction. In getting to know some of his associates, he discovered that they were making more money than he was. Although, by personal choice, he spent his lunch time working while his colleagues chatted over cocktails and enjoyed themselves at parties, he began to feel resentful at not receiving enough compensation for the long hours of work he invested in his firm.

Ignoring the possible reasons why they were making more money, why they were always smiling and making jokes, he speculated that either the boss favored them or they were involved in some subterranean illegal pursuits. In a state of doubt and suspicion, he decided to approach his boss. His boss explained that employees were treated equally and compensated according to seniority, and he reassured him that his performance was excellent. Mark felt relieved. He began to feel a bit more rational, grateful, and secure about his position: "I'm still young in the company, and evidently my associates have been with the company for many years. I have no control over them or their lifestyle. I like what I do. My boss is pleased with me. I need to be more patient." This sort of transition in his thoughts resulted in better feelings about himself and about his surroundings.

Often we need emotional strength and courage to deal with the dark demonic forces that threaten from within. It takes maturity and true manhood to work through inner despair and devastation. A man who harmonizes inner feelings with his logic gains greater strength and integrity with which to manage his life. He does not have to control all situations or the lives of others.

A male with a good image of self combines self-confidence, self-reliance, responsibility, and the willingness to defend his position or fight for his convictions with gentleness and warmth, as well as with the acceptance of the possibility of losing.

A man with a bad self-image focuses on infantile needs. He depends upon others for his existence and demands personal recognition and pampering. He becomes a passive-receptive receiver of bounties from others. Should he fail to receive, he feels defeated.

Men inherit multiple images, and like programmed computers, may be responding courageously in a composed, controlled, or even in a passive manner. Between the *masculine* behavior taught to young boys and the behavior expected of adult men, there may be cause for conflict and ambiguity.

Although conflicting images ensnare and paralyze the male mind, they are not absent in the female psyche. Inevitably, the impact that these images have is destructive to any human being. If they remain repressed, they will cause frustration and gradual emotional deterioration. If recognized and accepted as parts of the human dilemma, they undoubtedly will propel a person toward serious self-restoration or toward a competent psychotherapist who will assist in the process of reconstructing the self.

The male who is unable to deal with the ambiguities and conflicts imposed upon him resorts to defense mechanisms. He cannot comfortably deal with the full dimension of his personality and so allows himself to be one way at one time and another way at another time. Do you ever feel like a kaleidoscope, adopting changing images and styles? It feels uncomfortable.

Whether you are male or female, as a personal experiment try to be a realist. A realist sees things as they are and, therefore, is objective. Let us assume you are objective. You are capable of sizing up people and situations; you are honest in relating to others. Your words match your facial expressions, and you are the one who has the chance of healing ruptures, breaking impasses, or building bridges between people.

Looking more closely at this idea of the realistic male, in particular, as being the one who lives primarily in the present, we see that living realistically in the present gives joy and strength. To say, "I am a realist," is self-sustaining to everyone, but especially to a man.

Being a realist implies that you accept your own reality, the truth about who you are, whatever it may be. Safeguard this truth from outside forces. You do not need outside approval. No one really approves of an approval seeker. Letting go of the need for approval will clear the way for you to pursue the truth. More importantly, you need the truth so you can be in alignment with your inner self.

We live in an imperfect world, and like anyone else endowed with strengths and weaknesses, we are an indelible part of an imperfect life. Yet in an effort to restore the self, we try to monitor and improve our daily thoughts and actions, suspending the temptation to deceive ourselves and others with exaggerations. By doing good to overcome evil, we can internalize a code of good will and integrity that gives us inner peace.

Throughout history, people have searched for comfort and happiness — what the early Greeks called *eudaimonia* — meaning "good life," "prosperity." Until the present time, in spite of all our scientific and technological achievements, the observable data show most clearly that our search for *eudaimonia* has not produced results. With all our affluence, we are still a society of notoriously unhappy people: anxious, bored, critical, demanding, depressed, dependent, destructive, lonely. We resort to easy solutions: extramarital affairs, pornography, overeating, overdrinking, overworking, overrunning away from our impending fears of aging, sickness, and death. Or we join the fantasy world: daydreaming that things could be different and feeling depressed that they are not. Or we seek symbolic and superficial relationships.

For example, a guilty husband, in the vast majority of cases, will suffer from guilt knowing that he is breaking the promises that he so solemnly made. "Why should I feel guilty," he rationalizes, "when I merely indulge in a little harmless extracurricular activity? Many others are doing the same thing." To justify his affair, he may conveniently seek to find fault with his wife. "She's no longer attractive." "She is too busy with the children." "She's always tired."

If he listened to those pundits who claim that he owes it to himself "to have a full and active sex life," then he may reach the conclusion: "I'm a good provider, a good husband and father. I'm not going to break up my home, and as long as I hurt no one, I'm entitled to a good sex life."

Maslow, who utilized concepts such as "actualizing one's potential," "fear of one's greatness," and the "evasion of one's destiny," throws new light on the human dilemma:

> We fear our highest possibility, as well as our lowest ones. We are generally afraid to become that which we can glimpse in our most perfect moments.... We enjoy and even thrill to the godlike possibilities we see in ourselves in such peak moments. And yet we simultaneously shiver with weakness, awe, and fear before these very same possibilities.

To evaluate and effectively restore your self, it is important to recognize your emotional roadblocks. Without indulging in self-judgment, take a profound and gentle look at your inner strengths and weaknesses. Do you find that some of the qualities of your father or mother express themselves in you? Do you recognize these qualities? Have your parents' flaws become your flaws? Is your *negative self* really you, or is it a composite that you have learned from someone else, a person whom you once admired, a peer, relative, teacher, hero?

To some extent we are subjected to negative traits that serve a single purpose: they make us miserable. Unless the negativity is genetic, my hunch is that you learned it as you developed. You can relearn and attain new qualities that can be more productive for you. How? By involvement and practice.

If all automobiles were replaced by electric models, you would have no difficulty in learning new skills to operate an electric car. Necessity propels us into new discoveries. You will discover and devise new ways of dealing with life if you absolutely believe that you need a new approach. You would like to be happy, wouldn't you?

In business and industry, motivation is the difference between profit and loss, growth and stagnation. For your personal improvement, motivation can be the difference between success and failure, between emotional growth with fulfillment and mental deterioration, emotional death.

Ricky was a man motivated to change. He experienced a deprived and emotionally damaged childhood, quarrelsome parents who divorced when he was eleven. Ricky finally made it to college. He thought he had left behind the denigrating and dehumanizing images of his adolescent years when both father and mother thought of him as worthless. But when he brought home his first exam paper with a grade of 98, his father said, "What happened to the other two points?" His father negated the 98 points with his emphasis on the 2.

In spite of his father's negative attitude, Ricky felt an inner force that continued to motivate him to succeed. At college, he did well, and immediately upon graduation he found a job. A year later, he found his heart's first choice, Donna. He married her. The honeymoon and the overactive days of early marriage repressed Ricky's memory of his father's criticisms. As time passed, however, tensions returned: his fear of ambiguity and conflict tied in with early conditioning, pressures from home, pressures from peers, pressures, pressures. Marriage, which had appeared as a haven, now added more pressure to his life. It was difficult to function as mature husband, businessman, and person. He interpreted all things and happenings as good or bad, right or wrong, moral or immoral, crazy or sane. Ricky continually evaluated himself based on the missing 2 percent rather than on the 98 percent achieved.

This attitude prevented Ricky from having a flexible, open approach to life. He became rigid in his relationships, desiring to dominate or to be dominated. His inability to tolerate life's ambiguities and conflicts carried him to therapy. He did have a hard time dealing with the existence of haunting opposites and contradictions within, hostile feelings toward his parents, his inability to forgive their divorce, and fear that he, too, might end up in the divorce court.

Ricky invested time and money in his soul-searching and through therapy eventually arrived at a comfortable image of himself. He came to my office with a real smile one day. Besides sharing the joy of his thirty-third birthday, he wanted to continue his therapy and possibly increase the sessions to twice a week.

We set up the following goals to pursue in the sessions. Ricky must:

1. Focus on his reality as it is, both within and outside of his evolving self, no matter how unpleasant or difficult it might be. To do this he has to be fully aware of his strengths and weaknesses and accept them as his own. He has to confront his developing self and his life directly, honestly, using objective evaluations on the basis of facts.

2. Be flexible as he relates to his wife. Aware of his own nature, he has to be flexible enough to negotiate and treat other people with courtesy and concern.

3. Develop a healthier and happier relationship with his wife and his family of origin as well as with his in-laws.

4. Develop more courage to face difficulties in life and to remove roadblocks and obstacles. Primarily, he must confront life with patience and persistence, making good choices and facing consequences when he makes mistakes.

5. Express his feelings with a sense of maturity. When his feelings offend another person, he must consider the other's feelings and respond in a responsible way.

At the end of one session, Ricky said, "I want something from you; I want to copy that paragraph hanging on your wall."

"No problem — I'll give it to you," I said.

"It will be the anthem to my goal."

Nothing in the world can take the place of persistence.
Talent will not; nothing is more common than unsuccessful
    men with talent.
Genius will not; unrewarded genius is almost a proverb.
Education will not; the world is full of educated derelicts.
Persistency and determination alone are omnipotent.
The slogan "Press On" has solved and always will solve the
    problems of the human race.

— CALVIN COOLIDGE

For Your Consideration

~ Sit comfortably. Close your eyes. Breathe deeply and relax. Imagine a movie screen in front of you. The image on the screen is yours. See yourself in full dimension, working, walking, talking, playing, relating with others. You are alive and aware of all your motions, movements, and thoughts.

~ Think about what you see. Recognize aspects of your personality that you would like to change. State specifically when you plan to start the changing process.

~ Develop an interest in life that gives you inner satisfaction. It may be an interest in a person or a group of people, or an activity you enjoy such as reading or listening to music — the world is full of possibilities.

~ Keep your body in good health. Mass media advertisements bombard you with easy strategies and mechanisms to keep you physically fit. Each one has its own purpose. What is really of lasting value is as simple as taking a daily walk or visiting a friend.

~ In our fast-paced world where immediate satisfaction is an expectation, think of the potential of slowing down and relishing life. If you maintain a hurried pace, not only will you miss the scenery as you hasten by, but you might even miss the direction and purpose of your journey.

~ PART TWO ~

SELF-EXAMINATION

We cannot overlook the fact that there are differences among humans. What is of essence is how we perceive these differences. It is important not to consider our thoughts and decisions as absolutes. Men and women are endowed by God with a special nature, and it is a human function to fulfill this nature by obeying divine laws and logic.

Chapter 5

WHO AM I?

Everyone in therapy, or affected by therapeutic reflections even as diluted by the tears of TV-talk, is in search of an adequate biography: Who am I? How do I put together into a coherent image the pieces of my life? How do I find the basic plot?
— James Hillman

When you ask the question, "Who am I?" you might hesitate for half a second and then respond, "I am Carol." "I am Nancy." "I am Brent." "I am Stephen." Names, however, do not describe you as a person. You might say, "I am a computer programmer." "A banker." "A manager." "A teacher." "A mechanic." "A pilot." These may be descriptions of what you do, but again they don't describe you as a person. When you say, "I am loving." "Understanding." "Good." "Bad." "Intelligent." "Stupid." "Mean." "Controlling." "Judgmental" — the list could be endless — these adjectives describe your attitudes toward life. The more answers you give — such as "I am a mother," "I am a father," "I am married," "I am single," and so forth — the more aware you will become of the complexities of who you are. Like a polygon, your personality consists of many sides and many angles, although you are one and the same person.

Of course you are all in one piece. But as you stop and think about your self, you realize that it is a complicated entity. It is not really that *you* change. It is rather that you express different aspects of your self at different times. To state the matter simply, in the world theater you play different roles in different circumstances. What you probably don't know — and don't think of asking — is: Who chooses the role I play? If each aspect of your personality is an instrument of the same orchestra, who is the conductor? Who maintains the melody? Think of how many different aspects of your personality you have employed today in your encounters, at home, travel, work.

Vickie, in her early forties, had considered herself to be a good

daughter, wife, and mother. She centered her life on pleasing her fa-
ther, and later her husband, and finally her two children. She did
"all the right things." In the year following her fortieth birthday, she
started a career, got a divorce, and became, in her words, "a new
person." Then difficulties in relating with her teenage children arose.
They were confused and upset over their parents' divorce and angry
at their mother for spending her time in the activities of her new life.
Vickie herself was distressed and confused, for she found she was not
experiencing any feelings of love or caring for the children. "What
kind of a mother am I?" she thought and felt depressed. The words
"Who am I?" kept ringing in her ears.

Feeling guilty about her perceived selfishness, she withdrew from
her involvements, and for about six weeks she "fell back into the
old me." She was able then to feel love for her children, enjoy the
closeness, and experience relief until the moment when she raised the
question, "Should I be 'the old self' or the 'new self?'" Who can
honestly give the right answer?

It took Vickie a few months, with the help of a seasoned therapist,
to assess, accept, and integrate the many aspects of her personality
that she had previously repressed. She had to face her own reality and
work with parts of her self — her need for freedom and independence,
her striving to achieve her ambition, her desire to use her intellect,
her drive to compete, and so forth — and include them in her new
identity of being a strong, independent, intelligent person. Yet the
old self contained many important and valuable qualities: emotional
sensitivity and the ability to give and accept love. Subsequently, she
was able to see her situation not as an either/or process. Instead, she
developed a broader identity, which included aspects of both the old
self and the new self. A workable solution for Vickie was not to avoid,
ignore, or repress, aspects of her old self but to include the good parts
in the new self. Such a fusion can be considered a beginning of an
effort to restore one's self.

The above summarizes Vickie's story, but what does it all mean
for you? Take three deep breaths, exhale, close your eyes for thirty
seconds, and make the following affirmation:

~ I am who I am and I feel grateful to be alive.

~ I accept all aspects of my personality, although I don't under-
stand some of them.

~ I am willing to be selective with regard to these aspects and choose the better ones for a healthier, happier, and creative life.

With this simple beginning, you are getting a better picture of your self. Can you accept this picture as being the real you? Why not? This self that emerges with its spiritual dimension has the capacity to create any change that you can conceive to restore your self.

Granted, you cannot change the weather, the traffic, government policies, or major catastrophes in the world. When hard times come, adversity is a reality in life that none of us can escape, and you will need the wisdom to sustain your self and navigate through the shoals of adversity into a safe harbor. Whatever the state of your personality — be it timid, fearful, introverted, passive, extroverted, or aggressive — you can restore it.

"I can't help the way I am. I've always been this way," Linda said angrily to her daughter, Jennifer, who had, for the past six months, shut her mother out of her life. Perhaps unintentionally, she had controlled her daughter's new life by buying her furniture, telling her how to raise her children, how to run her home. Jennifer, the mother of three girls, wanted to establish a new identity with her husband and children, and for whatever reasons of her own, she did not appreciate her mother's frequent visits.

Linda, feeling excluded and depressed that her only daughter could not accept her as she was, kept looking for someone to agree with her that she was right and her daughter was wrong. But when a good friend said to her, "Stay out of your daughter's life," she fired back. "She only has one mother."

"Do you know anyone who has two mothers?" her friend asked, annoyed.

Linda's depression turned into endless tears and sleepless nights. Her family doctor prescribed medication, which she took for a few days and then discarded. "Nothing helps. I guess that's my nature. I take after my father; he was always depressed." She truly loved her father and came to believe that she had inherited those depressive feelings from him, and, therefore, they could not be overcome.

If we are to assume that Linda's condition was genetically determined, then she is a victim of her insidious belief in inheritance. A belief system like that does not allow any possibility for change. She can be enraged, cry, scream, and wallow in self-pity. It will not improve her situation one bit. She may need to take a profound look at her relationship with her daughter and realize the dangerous effects her anger can have on her self.

A more responsible response to her anger and its subsequent depression is to take charge of her self and make some new choices. It is up to her to commit herself to a process of change. She has to resist the temptation to insist on proving that she is right and her daughter is wrong and apply a new approach to connect with Jennifer. A good start would be to realize how damaging her anger is to her, a daily dose of poison, and let go of those angry feelings. She always has a choice concerning how to respond to her daughter's behavior. As an older and more experienced person, she should have a little more compassion for her young and inexperienced daughter. Linda's broken heart needed healing, and she had to see her self as being more than a physical being. She was also a spiritual reality. A spiritual shift can make the difference. The spirit within that keeps her alive can also guide, inspire, and point to a new and better direction, if she would only allow it. To initiate reconciliation, Linda has to stop focusing on her daughter's behavior and invest her energy in her husband and two sons. If Jennifer notices the changes in her mother — "she's off my back" — then she may respond better. With this kind of subtle reciprocity, their relationship may take a more positive turn.

Linda's depression lingered on for several weeks. She sought relief in food and ate more than necessary. Although she was aware that she was getting heavier, she reasoned, "I can't help it. It's my chemistry that requires more food. If I exercise, I'll lose weight." Nobody, not even a professional person, could convince Linda that it was not her chemistry that required more food. It was lack of confidence in her self that she could not change.

It was easy to blame Jennifer. She believed that her problem was caused by Jennifer's rejection of her. Linda actually convinced her self that her daughter was responsible for her depressive feelings. Could she know within her motherly heart that her daughter could not be totally responsible and that she had a choice? Could she really understand and admit that she, too, had contributed toward the deterioration of the mother-daughter relationship?

Jennifer's part was not totally innocent. Although a beautiful and happily married young woman, Jennifer was still angry with her mother. When she was eight, her mother had divorced her father, for reasons Jennifer never understood, and had married her high school sweetheart. In Jennifer's mind, her mother's choice to marry another man was unforgivable.

In scrutinizing Jennifer's attitude we can speculate that she was less damaged emotionally by the trauma of her parents' divorce when she was eight. She was more damaged by the traumatic way she remembered the experience — a time of externally caused calamities that wrongly shaped her character.

Interestingly enough, once she had a third child, she needed her mother's help and invited her to stay over at her house until her infant settled. Besides, she wanted her children to have a good relationship with their grandmother. Then she repressed her angry feelings and decided not to deal with them for the time being. One wonders if this was not her way of seeking to re-establish her relationship with her mother. Yet this was a very big step in her process of letting go of past hurts and making an effort to forgive her mother.

Of course Jennifer's mother was not aware of these underlying psychological reasons. She jumped at the opportunity of being with her daughter. She kept on being a doting grandmother, for she had learned a lot since Jennifer's childhood and was determined to be more loving with her grandchildren than she had known how to be with her daughter. She had learned to appreciate her daughter's quality of parenting and stopped interfering.

It takes two to make or break a relationship. When things are not going well, it does not help to point the finger and blame the other person. Rather, figure out what you can do differently to start a positive cycle and improve the relationship, if it is important to you. It takes only one person to open the possibility for the healing process. Someone must be brave enough take the first step.

Vickie's and Linda's stories, although not unique, are of persons who do not want to become victims of external forces. Somehow, you make a new beginning using the invisible part within you where you have choices to rid your self of toxic beliefs that stifle emotional growth. Simply, you cannot blame other things and other people for your personal state of mind.

Being unhappy, unmotivated, lazy, depressed — these and many other personality traits are a result of your thinking process. There are many people, including this writer, who have spent a large portion of their lives with very little in the way of material possessions and a whole lot of emotional deprivation. I grew up in a little village of four hundred families and had very limited means. With the exception of an old midwife, no medical personnel or medicine was available. I lived in a four-room house with five other members of the family including a stepmother and an emotionally unavailable father, no running water, no refrigerator, and no heating system. The educational system was primitive, and corporal punishment was the means of discipline for mischief or disobedience.

Four years of Nazi occupation not only terrorized the population with control, cruelty, and confiscation of food; it also caused three hundred deaths among a population of eighteen hundred people. Yet their habit was not to be depressed about their adverse fate. They attended church regularly, grateful to be alive; they celebrated life with its adversities, choosing a good spirit over despair.

This writer, a former barefooted olive-picker, found refuge in America. Initially, I washed dishes in exchange for food and a mediocre fee; I chose to attend school in the evenings. Working and going to school was not simply an arduous challenge; it was a great opportunity for growth and stability. Nothing came easily, but the motto "Press on" carried me through the alleys of doubt and opposing forces — "You cannot do this; you cannot do that; you'll never make it" — and sharpened my hope so I was able to pursue my dream, become self-reliant, and make a handsome life for myself and my family. Truly I am not bragging about my accomplishments. I am simply sharing a personal experience to reassure you of your potential. If I could do it, you can do it also.

So let's get rid of your negative traits and resistances. You possess one of the most powerful tools in the world: your mind. Observe it and watch its process. When you are awake, your mind continually produces thoughts. When you notice negative thinking, make a shift to something positive. Reframe your thoughts. If you did not want to see an ugly scene in a video, you would fast forward it to a pleasant scene. Do the same with pessimistic thoughts. Your mind can transfer you to a better part of your life. Listen no longer to external voices that are eager to pass on their wisdom to you and listen to your inner voice. Let the spirit in you do its work.

Just as you discard old clothes and put on new ones, abandon bad thoughts and habits and bring into your self new and creative thoughts and good habits. St. Paul's admonition fits perfectly in this area: "Let us abandon the works of darkness and put on the works of light... that we may walk prudently."

If you want to make a substantial difference in your life, then you must shift your inner self, that invisible part of you, from the state of wishing things were better for you to an intention of willingness to pay attention to whatever comes your way that will assist you in this effort. You are not a tree or a stone that is stationary and immovable. You can move and make the first step toward a healthier attitude. You are in charge now.

Realize that there is nothing to stop you from converting your thoughts to action. Better thoughts, more confident action. Aware of his sinful life, King David of the Old Testament prayed, "Create in me a clean heart, O God. Renew a right spirit within me." It is a clean heart and a renewed spirit that we need to realize who we really are so that unencumbered, we can continue the journey of life.

Wherever possible restore your violations, pay the penalty for whatever wrongs or injustices you may have caused, but also learn to leave behind you self-defeating attitudes instead of trying to justify their existence. You will be amazed at how quickly you can leave behind negative habits when you realize the results of positive response to your daily challenges.

For Your Consideration

~ When you wake up in the morning in a state of mental mist and you feel tired, unmotivated and directionless, obviously obstacles are in your way. You may feel unable to get out of your bedroom. You take a passive look in the mirror and ask, "Who am I?" Before you answer, start removing the obstacles that distort your image.

~ When you find yourself blaming others for your present life, it is good not to judge yourself harshly for not reaching your goal. Make it just a phase, not to be feared, but to serve a purpose. Your goal is to rediscover who you are. You will feel happier about yourself when you become less dependent, less demanding, less speedy, needy, and greedy.

~ Initially, blaming focuses on the injury and the injurer. Your feelings are not necessarily unjustified. Once you think through these feelings, as painful as they may be, then the tasks ahead become clear, and the possibility of forgiveness shines at the end of a once dark tunnel.

~ External voices will politely tell you that love is a high ideal, but one loaded with danger. There is a good chance that you will get hurt, so you should proceed cautiously. Don't give too much love because you may be taken advantage of. The question is, What does your own voice tell you? Take a risk and follow it.

Chapter 6

LEARN ABOUT YOUR SELF

―――――――――

Develop interest in life as you see it; in people, nature, things, literature, music — the world is so rich, simply throbbing with rich treasures, beautiful souls and interesting people.
— HENRY MILLER

IT IS A PSYCHOLOGICAL reality that most of us adopt personality characteristics of our parents. We emulate our parents, and in so doing we adopt their positive and negative qualities in return for both their positive and negative attention. Little boys try to imitate their fathers; little girls try to behave like their mothers. Every child at some time or other says or thinks, "I'm going to be like you when I grow up. Then you will always love me."

Adopting the negative traits is where the real trouble begins. If the mother is fearful, the child learns not to take risks. If the father is unemotional, the child learns not to show emotions. If both the mother and father have similar negative qualities, then the child gets a double dose of negativity.

The most negative attribute possible is the inability to love one's self or others. If our parents do not know how to love themselves and others, they cannot teach us how to give and receive love. Our parents' failure to teach us to love our selves and others properly is a major emotional roadblock in our lives.

Each of our parents somehow gives us some of the basic set of marbles with which we set out to play the game of life — some large marbles and others small, some round and smooth and beautifully colored, and others with slight discolorations or imperfections. Our childhood experiences in relating also teach us the rules by which we are to play the game. The strategies we use, however, are ours. For it is, most of all, how we respond to those experiences, and how we react to those rules that help to form us as we are.

Another factor influential in shaping our self-concept and patterns

54

of relating to others is our place in the family — whether we are the first child to come along, the middle, the last, or the only child. People are occasionally heard to remark about someone, "She's so different from her brother and from the rest of the family." It might seem at first thought that every child raised by the same parents would be similar in personality. Actually, however, every child born of the same parents is born into a different family altogether.

The first child may be born into a family of two parents with no rival for attention and affection. A second child is born into a family of two parents and an older brother or sister who reacts in a jealous way at the unexpected and unwelcome intrusion of another child into the family. The third child is born into a family of two siblings who have learned to live together and to whom the addition of another is no big deal. The various reactions each child experiences from each member of the family play a significant role in both telling the child who he or she is and how best to go about fitting in with others.

Let's return to you. From the time you began school, you discovered you were no longer the center of attention. You learned to work and play with a larger and more diverse group of human beings than before. You were confronted with a new and perhaps very different authority figure in the person of your teacher, and the way you learned to feel and think about your self and respond to others was further developed. Whether positive or negative, these attitudes and behavior patterns were internalized or modified. They were bound to be affected by the new environment — most especially by the way your peer group related to you.

Peer relationships were extremely significant in further helping to refine and redefine the way you as a child viewed yourself and others. With your peers, you learned to test the ideas and values given you by your parents, sometimes with results that were less than desirable. Where parental love and guidance were lacking, you as a growing child might have allowed yourself to be swayed and led by friends in ways that harmed you and others,

Early relationships can reinforce, or they can destroy even the most lovingly and carefully built psychological and moral foundations. It is this fact that causes parents so much concern about the kinds of friends their children have; they know that peer pressure and the need for peer acceptance are strong influences on any child, and not always for the child's good. Biblical wisdom claims: "Bad companions corrupt healthy morals."

An American Indian legend illustrates this point:

A brave found an eagle's egg and put it into the nest of a prairie chicken. The eaglet hatched with the brood of chicks and grew up with them.

All his life, the changeling eagle — thinking he was a prairie chicken — did what the prairie chickens did.

He scratched in the dirt for seeds and insects to eat. He clucked and cackled. And he flew in a brief thrashing of wings and flurry of feathers no more than a few feet off the ground. After all, that's how prairie chickens were supposed to fly.

Years passed. The changeling eagle grew very old. One day, he saw a magnificent bird far above him in the cloudless sky. Hanging with graceful majesty on the powerful wind currents, it soared with scarcely a beat of its strong golden wings.

"What a beautiful bird!" said the changeling eagle to his neighbor. "What is he?"

"That's an eagle, the chief of the birds," the neighbor clucked. "But don't give him a second thought. You could never be like him."

So the changeling eagle never gave him another thought. And he died thinking he was a prairie chicken.

It's all too easy going through life thinking you are a prairie chicken when you're really an eagle, but doing so shortchanges you and everyone else. Be what you are. Be all that you can be. Don't stay on the ground when you have it in you to soar.

Perhaps parents have constantly reminded you that you fall short of their expectations — or of your brother's or sister's or cousin's outstanding performance. No wonder, then, that you might tend to doubt yourself, as one of my depressed clients did.

Jean, a brilliant woman in her early thirties, unable to connect with the real world and make a decent living, lived a life of doubt and a me-myself-and-I narcissistic rage. It was not her fault that she was employed irregularly and in mediocre secretarial jobs which she hated and in which she felt mistreated by her employers. It was not her fault that she could not have a steady relationship with a man. She blamed others for her lack of success. Obviously she could not leave behind her the *fury* of blame. A love-hate relationship with her mother held her prisoner of the past. She still lived at home, ever reminded of her mother's unfulfilled expectations, and she felt guilty.

Her mother wanted her to become a teacher like her sister's daughter, who was now a happy high school principal. But Jean did not want to hear about that. Halfway through her college program, she dropped out and joined a theater group. She had hopes of becoming an actress and auditioned at every opportunity; however, she was not even considered for a small part in any type of production. Her dreams of stardom withered away.

From a very early age, therefore, and in more profound ways than you might have imagined, your own image of your self, of the world, and of others has been colored by the way significant people in your life have related to you. If those relationships have primarily been positive ones, then you most probably have good feelings about your self and your life and find it easier to relate to others. If, on the other hand, you have been denied these positive relationships as a small child, you are more likely to find it difficult now to accept your self, to cope with life, or to relate well with others.

Lynn, a tragic victim of a lie, wallowed in self-pity and destructive passivity. At twenty-nine she had no job, no desire to read the newspaper, no strength to fill out an application. Her weekly allowance from her grandmother was hardly sufficient to buy enough liquor. So far as having a boyfriend, she had had a few unsuccessful experiences. "Men cannot be trusted anyhow! They are only after one thing," she claimed. In her effort to avoid pain, she kept saying, "I know I can do it. One day I'll get out of this mess." Again back to alcohol and numbness — a coping device that she began to employ at nineteen.

At the age of eight, Lynn discovered that the man who used to visit her mother was not really her uncle. He was her mother's lover. Lynn grew up in an atmosphere where her mother, overwhelmed by her affair, could not adequately fulfill a maternal role. Lynn felt inferior and unlovable. However, she received love and affection from her paternal grandmother, who thought that little Lynn would grow up to be as educated as her father. She would be a doctor or a lawyer — a professional woman. Later in life, when she felt unable to carry the burden of her grandmother's aspirations, which had become her own, Lynn accepted the perception of her self that she thought her mother had of her: inferior and unlovable. These two images produced doubt and discomfort, which alcohol pacified.

Lynn's inner turmoil, as she grew up in a hostile home where her parents' marriage ended in a nasty divorce, was later compounded when she permitted a married man to come and live with her. He shuttled between his wife and Lynn's apartment. After the romance subsided, he treated her just as her mother had done, irresponsibly and uncaringly.

Reenactment of childhood conditions is a common circumstance that affects our adult life. Lynn's psychological memory was her worst enemy. Remembering the *big lie,* old humiliation, insult to her pride, she felt fragmented. In therapy, she held on to her hurt feelings as if they were priceless works of art to be displayed on the wall of her mind. She clung passionately to her child's perception of parental injustice, so her image of her self was distorted by anger and eagerness for revenge. Her world was ugly, and life was not worth living.

It took several weeks of intense psychotherapy before Lynn drew her own inferences about her self. "I have no control over what happened to me in childhood. Blaming my mother is an easy way to stay where I am and promote my own false importance over her. As long as I continue the blaming, I'll never have enough energy left to engage in anything worthwhile for my self."

Gradually Lynn gave up alcohol and blame and converted her inner conflicts into creativity. She dropped the married man, joined AA and attended three meetings per week, and eventually got herself a job. She also enrolled in evening classes where she studied marketing skills. There was a drastic improvement in how she felt about her self. The fragments were pieced together, making a new design and creating for Lynn a healthier self-image. Now her task was to maintain a more responsible attitude toward her life. She no longer collected an allowance from her grandmother, bringing an end to dependency needs. Her personality resources were enhanced through education and activities. She abandoned unrealistic goals and coordinated her ambitions within her capacities. Lynn exhibited a desire to cultivate and to restore the once-malfunctioning self.

This is why "restoration" is such a good word. As if we were rehabilitating a piece of furniture and discovered under the exterior a superb and valuable original, our aim is to bring the real self out. Our self is the central core within each of us, unique and distinctive, where the power cells of growth reside. To operate without a good solid contact with that power source of your inner self is to be out of synchronization. To function in harmony is to be a creative, contributing person with a deep sense of well-being.

For Your Consideration

~ You know your self better than anyone else does. You probably know your qualities and potentialities best; you are certainly the only one who can explore and develop them.

~ Your perception of your feelings, attitudes, and ideas matters far more than any outside diagnosis. Your self-image determines your behavior.

~ Your present behavior can be understood only from your point of view. If you cannot accept your present behavior, much of your energy will be spent defending it instead of analyzing and improving it.

~ You do want to know about your true self. If you didn't, you would not be reading this book. No one can force you to alter and enhance your life. You will do it when you feel ready or sense the need to be free and willing to put your own resources to work.

~ As you begin to mature and actualize your self, you will also begin to interact more enjoyably with other people. Your respect for your individuality and acceptance of your self as a person of unique worth will make the restoration process easier, filled with the joy of discovery.

Chapter 7

EXPRESS YOUR SELF

To express our feelings in a more meaningful way we must focus into them and get in touch with what is in us. These feelings may relate to how you interact with other people, but they will be strictly your own feelings.
       — EUGENE T. GLENDIN

As YOU READ these lines, take a risk and express your self. Rest assured that no part of this effort is designed to judge you or intimidate you. The objective of this book is to help you restore your self. In spite of weaknesses or feelings of insecurity, you will discover ways to approach life with the confidence you need to become the best you can be. Many of us have difficulty in expressing ourselves, or we become hindered by doubt of our own potential. We fear that we might be wrong or misunderstood, criticized, judged, or even punished, and we keep silent or say what others like to hear, lest we lose their friendship.

Expressing exactly how we feel about another person or situation or any issue in life implies that we take a risk — perhaps a calculated risk. If we feel good about ourselves, we speak with confidence when describing an idea, stating an opinion, or responding to a request. We experience a freedom to make our presence known to another person or to a group. If our self-esteem is low or our self-image is tarnished by past experience and we feel deprived, we prefer to withdraw, remain silent, or repress how we feel lest someone notice the part of our self that we are unhappy about.

At this junction in your life, as you start a personal inventory, you may have serious questions. Gently and with compassion, review your life. Without judgment or condemnation, raise the question: What is my self-image?

A self-image is what your mind's eye perceives as you. It is purely a mental representation. For example, close your eyes and visualize your mother. She may not be present, but her image is with you; it stands for her. The image is obviously based on the memory traces of previous perceptions of your mother. Because you have an image of her, your mother acquires a psychological reality that is not tied to her physical presence. An image is a reflection. It is not a complete reality.

An image not only re-evokes what is not present, but also enables a human being to retain an emotional connection with an absent object. The image of your mother may evoke the love you feel for her, or the hate; even after her death, her image remains with you, and so do your feelings for her. An image becomes a substitute for the external object. It is actually an inner experience, that is, a product of your mind.

Infants cannot form images for the first six to seven months. By the eighth month or soon after, the infant is able to have images. Images begin to constitute the foundation of the inner reality, which in human development is as important as external reality, possibly more.

The countless images that have been filed in your mind's archives shape and form the image that you have about your self and the world around you. At times, you may want to remove your self from reality; you may want to have an alternative. It is then that you visualize things in different ways.

Attaining an image of your choice may be an attempt to gratify a longing for that which is not available, and it may also be a springboard to creativity. If you imagine something desirable that exists but that is not available, you may be motivated to act, to search, and to find the desired object. If the desired object does not exist, you may be motivated to create it. If you cannot find it or create it, you may daydream about it. As you turn your attention toward your self, do not think of a self-centered person. If you don't know your self, if you don't think and take care of your self, who will? If your self is tormented or fragmented, how can it be of use to anyone? Moment by moment, you must make claims upon life, monitor your experiences, attend to sensory impressions, experience your body and its functions, your mind and its thoughts. This is the way to rediscover and restore your self. Your triumphs and your failures are all yours. Each discovery is an aspect of your personality.

There will be aspects of your self that puzzle you, as well as aspects which have long been buried, seemingly forgotten. Putting the pieces of the puzzle together will be a redefinition of your self-image. How you look, what you say, what you think and do, what you feel and believe at this very moment — all this is you. This is the image that you have defined.

Each of us is created with a potentially healthy self-image that, in time, may have suffered some trauma. Besides experiencing the physical environment, we experience an emotional climate provided by our family, siblings, relatives, and later by society. All influences are internalized, organized, and reorganized to bring balance to our life.

Some of us are surrounded by potentially supporting, caring, and even loving people who validate our presence. If we accept that we are born into groups of people — parents, siblings, and friends — who may genuinely accept us and show us warm empathy and care, then we are not alone. We may develop the courage not only to recognize this group, but also actively and joyfully to participate in it and live a productive life.

However, there are others who feel unwanted, unaccepted, alienated, unconnected, molested, traumatized, or isolated. How long has this gone on? When was the bond of belonging broken?

Stacy was strapped by her arms and legs to a hospital bed. Sedated, blue marks around her left arm, an intravenous needle in her wrist, she could hardly whisper or open her eyes. This was her second attempt at committing suicide over the betrayal of a boyfriend. She had been intimate with him, for she viewed the relationship as serious, leading to marriage. Then she discovered he was married. He admitted to her over the phone that their affair was a mistake and that he had no intention of leaving his wife. Stacy's mother was not at home, when in a moment of sheer rage, Stacy swallowed a bottle of Advil pills. Luckily, a neighbor who dropped in to see her mother found Stacy groaning on the floor.

Both her doctor and the hospital would not release her until an appointment had been made with a local therapist. I accepted the call, and her mother came first to my office.

On the brink of hysteria, her mother said tearfully, "Not again! She probably misses her father; he died twenty years ago, and I had to do everything for this girl all by myself. I paid for her education, and I must say she excelled as a student; I always gave her an allowance, bought whatever she wanted, took her on vacations. I provided well for her. Now I'm at a loss. I don't know what else I can do."

My instant reaction was to say to this worried mother, "There is nothing else that you can do. Perhaps you should stop being her rescuer." But I'm not in the habit of making a quick diagnosis. In an effort to be of some help, I listened to the mother's words of frustration, wondering and speculating how she had contributed to her daughter's condition.

Stacy entered my office hesitantly. She had a statuesque body, six feet tall. She was attractive and beautifully dressed. Any man would find it a challenge to date her; but she was not available. She had had a couple of long-term relationships that turned out to be very disappointing. "Men cannot really be trusted," was a nagging thought. To fill the gap of her loneliness, the Internet provided her with hours of dialogue and entertainment. Meeting people online from other countries fascinated her. In terms of work, although she was a college graduate, she could not get a decent job. Her employment usually lasted from about six months to a year, which was long enough to permit her to apply for short-term unemployment benefits. She had the idea that someday she would have her own business, possibly a fancy boutique at the Short Hills Mall in New Jersey. Her mother subsidized her and paid her overdue credit card accounts.

Stacy had a history of being bored, dissatisfied, and unable to connect with the real world; with the exception of two girlfriends, former classmates, she had little contact with anyone. The three friends met occasionally on the weekend and sat around drinking wine, talking about men, discussing the latest fashions, and planning future vacations at exotic resorts.

Stacy spent an uneventful twenty-seventh birthday at home with her mother. The previous week she had met a handsome man a few years younger than herself, and they had an interesting conversation. She was somewhat obsessed with him and wanted to phone him, but she was afraid he might think she was being too aggressive. She was preoccupied with conflicting thoughts and feelings about previous failed relationships with men. Her father was the first major loss in her life. Later, the loss of boyfriends precipitated a real fear of male relationships and provided the groundwork for additional pain. Should she risk another relationship? Stacy had a difficult time seeing beyond her emotional and physical needs and the immediacy of her current sense of dissatisfaction. How should she behave? That depends. Could she come to terms with what it means to be human? Could she explore the possibility of being honest with her self? Could she be wiser in her choices? Could she put another person's well-being before her own? Could she be loving?

Stacy was confronted with a challenge — and so was I. She had to answer those questions honestly. My part was to provide guidelines, as well as a warm therapeutic environment where Stacy could feel she was accepted and understood. My office had to be the haven where she could feel safe and protected from her own destructive impulses. The challenge she had to face was not grieving over losing boyfriends but looking deeper into her self, where the root of the problem lay. She lost the man she was hoping to marry; we all know that a loss cannot be underestimated or replaced easily. Current losses always sent her back to her major and irreplaceable loss, which was the death of her father. He died of a rare type of cancer of the spine before his fiftieth birthday, when Stacy was only seven. She cried then, but her mother's loving presence always soothed her wound and helped her to adjust.

Later in life, when she attended a girlfriend's wedding, she broke down with endless tears. She saw the happy bride escorted down the aisle by a proud daddy and really felt the absence of her own father. "That is something I cannot have. I have no father." She admitted to no one the cause of her tears. The experience threw her into a state of depression.

In search of resolution, the conscious and unconscious mind perpetually conspire to provide answers, which at times are not even rational. Yet they serve a purpose in that they challenge the suffering soul to pursue healing.

The experience of loss, which was one of the causes of Stacy's depression, generated a sense of helplessness, which, in turn, made her feel hopeless and worthless. Added to that were the lingering feelings of double anger — anger at her father who died leaving her unprotected, and anger at her mother for not preventing her father's death. She was even angry at the world for not making her happy. She decided to end it all. "Make my survivors suffer their loss."

It was evident that Stacy was a tormented soul. Then came the questions: Was suicide an attempt to liberate her soul from the neurotic perceptions of her self and the world around her? Was it her way of destroying her self for feeling worthless? Of course she needed to look deeper into her self and rediscover the part that was still healthy.

Regardless of what your reality is, pleasurable or painful, active choices are necessary for growth. This may lead you to take chances and utilize aspects of your personality that have been dormant or repressed. Restoring your self may include reaching within, reaching out, connecting with others, and developing new relationships. You need to find friends who can be nurturing and supportive. Avoid people who are depressed or stagnant; they may drag you down and infect you with depressive feelings. You need upbeat individuals who are active and enthusiastic about life. They can instill a joyful spirit in you, if you allow them.

There will come a time when, with a restored self, you will be able to show compassion and understanding for others. Redefining your self implies deep and meaningful contact with the outside world. The depth and breadth of your experience will be developed through empathy: suffer with those who suffer, rejoice with those who are joyful, be reborn each spring. We come away from each experience, joyful or painful, with greater sensitivity and understanding. We feel the impact of birth, love, anger, illness, death, resurrection. We share in the exhilaration of young love, the companionship of old age, the anguish of the plutocrat's search for pleasure and more wealth. We understand ghetto despair and the hopelessness of the alienated.

The way we relate to others is largely influenced by the way we think of ourselves. Our self-concept is, in turn, the result of many influences. In learning to relate, it is important that we first identify these influences and understand how they have helped to determine who we now are and how we relate to others.

Of particular importance in restoring your self is your relationship with your parents. The way you see your self now is due in large part to the perception you were given of your self by your parents. From infancy, you were given messages about who you were and what you were like. Someone's consistently affectionate touch or impatient handling told you from the beginning whether or not you were lovable and loved. As you grew old enough to understand language, you might have overheard words such as, "He's the aggressive one," or "She's the generous one in the family." You were sometimes hugged and sometimes spanked. However you experienced these things, they taught you your first lessons about your self and how others saw you. Your responses formed the basis for your present self-image.

For Your Consideration

~ Express your self creatively and honestly. Each attempt will result in further self-expression and joyous discovery.

~ Learn to be in touch with the silent part of your self, your soul. Everything you need to know about your life lies within.

~ Nothing out there can control what is within you. It is the other way around. As you think so shall you be. Your thinking is yours, it originates with you, and it precipitates good or bad feelings about your self and the world around you. The society in which you live is simply the stage upon which you perform. The quality of your performance depends upon how you feel.

~ If you live a life of fear and doubt, it will be difficult to restore your self. Fear and doubt hold you back from doing something good and of benefit to your self. In a state of inertia when you find your self blindly obeying fear and doubt, you can change those negative feelings by trusting the force that flows throughout your being.

~ Rather than being critical about what you observe in your self now, you should look to what you might truly like to enjoy in your personality. Visualize a level of confidence that you would like to exhibit as you encounter and interact with other people in all walks of life. Would you like to be less timid and more assertive? Would you like to be less angry and more gentle and loving? Would you like to be less passive and more creative? It is possible. Create in your mind an image of your self that serves you best and move on.

Chapter 8

THE TRUTH ABOUT YOUR SELF

It is fascinating to be a human being, and each of us is a miracle. In the magnificent, complex architecture of life on this planet, human life is like the rising sun. The glorious essence of human being is always present within each of us, just like the sun, even though sometimes it cannot be seen. To reach it, we need to work on overcoming what stands in between. — BHANTE Y. WIMALA

IT IS YOUR BIRTHRIGHT to be a happy person. Within you lie all the ingredients for a meaningful and enjoyable life. If your life is hectic and currently disturbed by what is or has been happening to you, your inner essence will help to restore your self.

When you were young, you were innocent and pure, spontaneous and active, curious and eager, loving and lovable. When you became an adult, these qualities may have been veiled by a world that was not as supportive as it was when you were young. However, if you allow your heart to be open and if you use the practical material explained in this book, you will rediscover your youthful qualities: happiness, eagerness, curiosity, kindness, and desire for personal growth. These attributes are God's gift to humans.

Worldly happiness is easily understood and, in reality, everyone wants to be happy. This is a normal human condition. However, sometimes happiness is external. Gadgets and material wealth may make you happy. The question is: For how long? It is important to realize that inner joy is of greater value than external happiness. This is attainable if we decide to use the enormous capacity of our minds.

The human mind has given birth to all the marvels and accomplishments of our evolving civilization. It has also contributed to man's inhumanity to man, exploitation, wars, moral deterioration, and destruction. How we use the unique gift of our mind makes all the difference. It is time to renew our mind's soulful search for happiness and fulfillment, to begin afresh our journey toward finding what really matters in life. How do we make our life into something worth living? How do we find our true selves and learn to live and to love better? We can reclaim our God-given gift of the wholesome qualities that may be dormant or partially submerged. The twin within, the spiritual part of our self, possesses extraordinary power for recovery and growth.

In an age of rapid, almost frantic change, the quality of individual as well as of family life has been radically affected. Value systems are in conflict, the future is confusing and therefore threatening, the stability of all institutions seems compromised, and lifestyles come into vogue and quickly pass. In this general absence of continuity, life becomes increasingly unpredictable as the familiar landmarks, clouded by mass media confusion, disappear from view. This may explain, in part, our increased interest in psychological investigation and our search for the ideal therapist, our passionate obsession with self-scrutiny and our search for self-awareness. All are evidence of our perpetual quest for purpose and meaning in life.

In contrast to our counterparts of two or three generations ago, our field of knowledge is awesome; Internet technology and modern communication have brought vast new worlds of information and experience within our ken. Yet there is a great feeling of emptiness and emotional deprivation pervading our society. It seems that the more we learn about our selves, the less we think of our selves. We tend to feel inferior and unaccomplished. Perhaps the observation is valid, that the more one observes life, the less one participates in living. Let's narrow the focus to see how this observation applies to you.

How you feel about your self determines, in large part, how you see the world around you and how you respond to it. How you see and feel about your self directly affects how you relate to others. For example, if you've developed the feeling you're no good or not good enough, you will hesitate to seek out others as friends. After all, friendship is a gift of self, and who wants to give something that might be found defective? So you tend, even if obliquely, to repel other people's overtures of friendship because you feel unworthy.

It is more than likely that not too many offers of friendship will be made, for if you see your self as weak and needy, others will also see you as a dependent person. If you see your self as riddled with problems with which you have difficulty coping, others will likewise size you up as a "helpee," with whom friendship tends to be one-sided.

If, on the other hand, you see yourself as a maturing person — a person with adult aspirations and not someone mired down in negativism — then you will be willing to take the initiative in establishing and sustaining interpersonal relationships.

Feel good about whatever strengths you possess. For instance, if you know yourself to be a caring person, then you don't need the constant reassurance of comparison to others for validation of this quality. Instead, you're free both to present yourself as you are and to accept others as they are. All our absurd human foibles have their roots in the absence of self-assurance.

The male who feels insecure about his masculinity develops a ridiculous macho style. He adopts a Don Juan attitude toward women and tries to manipulate them as objects for conquest, thus missing the more pleasurable involvement with them as persons. It's no different with the female who is unsure of her femininity and engages in all sorts of fatuous coquetry. So your self-concept greatly influences your style and how you express your self.

At the deeper level, the way you perceive your individual self tends to shape your definition of what kind of a person you are and the kind you ought to be. It's no wonder the ancient Greeks put one idea ahead of all the others: *Know thyself.*

We talk ponderously about the dilemma of contemporary times and feel pressured to adjust. Having made the atom yield its secrets, having probed deeply into outer space, having prodigiously increased our knowledge of planets and stars, we have shrunk our universe — or so we suppose — to manageable proportions. In so doing, we seem also to have reduced our selves and diminished our sense of being central to the universe; no longer do we see our selves as the Psalmist saw us: "a little less than God." It's interesting to note that the Greek word for atom, *atomon,* also means "the individual." Literally, it means "that which is indivisible, the irreducible." In other terms, for the understanding of life, humans are the ultimate reality. We come to terms with our world once we have come to terms with our own humanity — all its weaknesses, all its splendid possibilities. Exploring the possibilities almost always necessitates change.

Change is always fraught with risk. Reaching for the unknown can be frightening. Whenever we try to change some aspect of our life, we feel uncertainty. But, like the giant oil rig probing the seabed, it is only by reaching into the unknown that there is any hope of discovery. Maturing and growing older involve changing. To resist change is to arrest development. In order to grow, the lobster has to shed its shell many times. Each time it sheds, the creature is totally defenseless until the new shell forms. Nature gives us this lesson in a myriad of ways. It is no different with us: from infancy to adulthood, every phase of our lives demands change, and during the process of change, we are vulnerable.

The challenge of our personal growth may be threatening. We may fear growth because it often means abandoning some of our familiar or even infantile needs and neurotic patterns in order to achieve the unknown. In his book *Neurosis and Treatment: A Holistic Theory*, Andras Angyal states:

> Abandoning the familiar for the unknown always involves risks. When the changes are far-reaching or precipitous, they are bound to arouse anxiety. The view that growth is insepara- ble from anxiety is shared by practically all thinkers who have substantially contributed to our understanding of anxiety.

This may be the reason you are reading this book. You may be looking for a change. You *wish* your situation were different: that you had more time or money, that you were older or younger, that you were married or single, and so forth. Your only real option is to face what *is* and to focus on what you *can do* to change it, if in reality it can and ought to be changed. And invariably there is risk. But if risk inhibits, remember the lobster: vulnerability is the price of growth.

If you and I share with the Psalmist his wonder that humans were fashioned "a little less than God," surely we must try to understand what it is that constitutes our humanity and how, having been made in the image of our Creator, we can more nearly approximate the likeness. We can become creators of a better life. It is the creative potential within us that is the image of God. At this hour, the most distinctive thing about you is your body. You can accept your body as beautiful, strong, useful, a source of pleasure; you want to develop it and keep it healthy. When you discover the marvelous properties of your mind, your capacity to inquire and create, you will cultivate them. You will be enchanted by their unlimited potential.

There are additional attributes that seem to link us even more closely to our divine origins. When we come to know the power of true love, when we sense the sovereignty of truth, when we perceive the moral rightness and wrongness of things, then we will recognize the unique place we occupy in the scheme of life. Humanity does not mean masses of people; it describes what each of us possesses as a divine gift, to be treasured, developed, and refined.

Is there some way, constant and reliable, to measure your humanity, to determine whether and to what extent you are an authentic human being? Is there an absolute standard? Of course not. Each of us is unique. Yet there are certain attributes by which your full humanity can be authenticated. You are independent. This is fundamental — the essential gift of freedom. You are creative. You can be loving, truthful, honest with your self as with others.

You possess judgment to know when change is called for and to recognize and assess its risks, to adapt to the new and to keep what is useful and valuable in the old and discard what is not. You cherish your physical health and seek your mental and emotional well-being. You are not reluctant to feel and to express what you feel; you do not withhold your love and friendship, but you will not turn away from a fair fight. You are equally comfortable with tenderness and toughness. Above all, you will be a goal-setter and goal-attainer. In short, you are not static but dynamic, a growing creature, exploring the unknown, maturing each moment.

For Your Consideration

~ Be who you really are and then do what you need to do in order to have what you want. Open your self to the possibility of other dimensions of reality that are available to you. What you are familiar with is the energy and the strength of your body. Parallel to your physical reality is the potential of your spirit, your soul.

~ Whatever it is to know or accomplish in your life, believe and trust your inner qualities and be patient. The spirit within will reveal and make it available to you. When you stop hearing external voices and silence your thoughts, your soul will seek whatever is good and beneficial for your happiness.

~ One of the most common causes of failure to have whatever we wish is the attitude of negativity that manifests itself in the following type of thinking: "It's unlikely that I'll get that job unless I know somebody with power. What I'm trying to do is beyond my capabilities. Others have tried and failed. Life is full of problems. I'm not much good at anything." When life becomes difficult and hazy, who is going to help you? Only your own friend within. Your spirit will say, "I am here; why are you worried?" To establish this friendship, you have to be aware of that friend, aware and confident that you have a friend within. Then you will never be lonely.

~ Visualize life as a journey. Keep your destination clearly in mind, and at the same time try to enjoy all the beautiful scenery along the way. If life starts taking you in a different direction where in reality you don't want to go, be willing to change your destination. Don't be eager to arrive. Relax, be firm, yet flexible, and enjoy the experience.

~ Be patient. It has taken you a lifetime to create your world the way it is now. It may not necessarily change instantly, although sometimes it does. With perseverance and a proper understanding of your efforts, you will succeed in creating what seem like many miracles in your life.

~ PART THREE ~

SELF-EVALUATION

Humans have made many strides in all areas of existence. Many advances. Many improvements. But in our basic human concerns, there is little change from the very beginning of recorded history until the present. Our true selves do not need to change; they need to be liberated from destructive forces.

Chapter 9

CHANGING TIMES — CHANGING PEOPLE

*Because of the constant change and the feeling of being "off bal-
ance" it is essential for men and women to develop . . . coping
skills and accept this as all right. . . . Choose priorities and spend
time relaxing and enjoying life, in spite of all that needs to
be done.* — BRUCE A. BALDWIN

MONICA WAS IN A PIVOTAL moment in her relationship with Matthew.
She had enjoyed his company for eight months. She perceived Mat-
thew as a good, generous, and honest man who loved her. "He's fun
to be with, he respects me, and he makes me laugh," she claimed.
However, they had never spoken to each other of their emotions.
She felt a strong need for self-expression and for clarification of his
feelings for her. How should she approach the subject? She might
demurely admit that she was attracted, stimulated, fascinated, or in-
trigued by him. More boldly, she could say she was infatuated or was
falling in love with him. Taking a greater risk, she could say that he
made her intoxicated or madly passionate.

Monica held back other emotions. She was a mature woman who
wanted a man in her life, one totally devoted to their relationship.
At that delicate moment, how could she use such terms as "want,"
"need," and "love"? As a spiritual person, she valued that unseen part
of her self, her soul. Aware that any relationship required balance,
she monitored her emotions, lest she drive Matthew away.

Matthew was of the Jewish faith. Although he did not attend the
temple frequently, he observed major holy days with his parents.
Monica was a Christian and attended church every Sunday. Could
the strong convictions of her faith in Jesus Christ separate her from
the social consequences that might result if she married Matthew and
had a family?

Living life fully and having the man she loved in her life was a welcome challenge, and Monica, an attractive brunette from New Jersey and a professional woman, expressed her emotions to Matthew with confidence. Her church environment encouraged the spirit of faith, hope, and charity. Recently, she had learned that God in His abundant love does not impose His grace upon people. He requires their consent. She came to the realization that it was not fair to expect Matthew to adopt her faith and become a member of her church. She knew that in practicing her faith, she might indirectly influence Matthew to start attending the temple. She respected his faith and began to read about Judaism.

Monica and Matthew reached a mutual agreement: Their relationship was important and it needed to be nurtured by commitment to fidelity, honesty, love, and faith in God. Some spirituality in their life could be a source of strength, and they agreed that each of them had to look into their individual faiths for guidance and share the outcome with each other. They pledged respect for each other's faith and promised not to be critical of each other's religious practices.

Monica was pleasantly impressed one day when Matthew announced that he had decided to join Beth Miriam Temple, which was only five blocks from his apartment. One Friday evening when they met for dinner, he brought her a small scroll on which were several paragraphs written in calligraphy; the rabbi had given a copy to each member of his congregation. "Read it to me," Monica said.

Matthew looked at her with a tender smile, and began to read.

Truth is one; sages call it by various names.
It is one sun which reflects in all ponds.
It is the one water which slakes the thirst of all.
It is the one air which sustains all life.
It is the one fire which shines in all houses.
Colors of the cows may be different, but milk is white.
Flowers and bees may be different, but honey is the same.
Systems of faith may be different, but God is one.
As the rain dropping from the sky wends its way toward
    the ocean,
so the prayers offered in all faiths reach the one God,
Who is supreme.

"Beautiful!" Monica said. "One light, many colors; one water, many thirsts; one essence, many shapes of humans." She reached out and held his hand. "And we are all connected by one God who loves us."

"It is a good feeling," said Matthew.

The following Sunday, Monica shared a passage of St. Paul from his First Epistle to the Corinthians, chapter 13:1–8, on which her pastor based his sermon, The Gift of Love.

> If I could speak in the tongues of people and of angels, but do not have love, I am a noisy gong or a clanging cymbal. And if I could have prophetic powers, and understand all mysteries and all knowledge, if I could have all faith, so as to remove mountains, but do not have love, I am nothing.... Love is patient; love is kind; love is not envious or boastful or arrogant or rude. It does not insist on its own way; it is not irritable or resentful; it does not rejoice in wrongdoing, but rejoices in the truth. It bears all things, believes all things, hopes all things, endures all things. Love never fails.

"That's the best definition of love I have ever heard," Matthew said.

"Maybe someday when we get married we can use it," Monica said.

"I think we should frame it and hang it in a prominent place," Matthew replied.

In a subsequent meeting they spoke about their future together. Although they spoke of the possibility of getting married, developing their careers was their priority. Marriage could wait, they thought, and they decided to see each other only once a week. Both agreed to give each other personal time and space for growth and self-fulfillment. Matthew pursued a political career, a dream that he had entertained since college years. Monica, on the other hand, had finished her internship as a physical therapist and was pursuing research work in holistic medicine.

A year later: As their life unfolded in an increasingly high-tech society, a degree of saturation began to affect their relationship. Their simplified yet satisfying way of communicating began to suffer as they moved on with their busy schedules. The once a week face-to-face intimate dialogues in the dining-living-bedroom dwindled to random moments from their busy life.

After a day in her office, Monica returned home to find her mailbox stuffed with correspondence — advertisements, mail-order catalogues, offers of immediate house-improvement loans, bills, and letters.

She checked her voice mail to find it inundated with messages to be returned; some were urgent and needed immediate attention.

She tried to arrange a meeting with a colleague to discuss a serious case of a patient whom they were treating cooperatively, but she was attending a conference in Europe. An attempt to reach her on her cellular phone failed.

As she was reading her e-mail and thinking about the next morning's 8:00 o'clock staff meeting at the hospital, her phone rang. A friend who had just flown in from Los Angeles called from the airport and wanted to meet with her for breakfast the following morning.

On that same evening, Matthew surprised the woman he loved with a brief visit. After an intimate hug and a prolonged kiss, he was eager to share his enthusiasm over a political dinner in his honor. Although Monica wanted to listen, she felt overwhelmed by the day's routine. She yawned, and Matthew felt unappreciated. Both felt tired and annoyed; they silently withdrew from each other. Matthew wanted to leave, but Monica persuaded him to stay. After a long silence, they admitted that external pressures were dominating their life. They relaxed during the weekend and decided to take time out to discuss their life seriously.

Monica started with a smile. "I don't want us to have a microwave relationship." Matthew was not clear what she meant, and Monica went on to say, "I don't like our life the way it is. Some days I would like to have the traditional family — you know, a provider father, a caretaking mother, children whose lives would be centered in the home until early adulthood."

"I would love that too," Matthew said, "but is that realistic for us at this time? We both work and have relations and responsibilities outside the home. If we had children, baby-sitting facilities would be required. Eventually they would need to be driven to day-care centers and then to school and after-school activities. There would be parent-teacher meetings to attend."

"You're right. We need to give all that some thought, but we need to have balance in our life. We need accountability toward each other and responsibility for our relationship. What I mean is, I don't want our home to be a pit stop; I'd rather see us have a nesting place. In spite of our affluence, I would hate to give up the traditional image of the close-knit family."

After serious self-examination and re-evaluation of their rela-
tionship, both Monica and Matthew made a concerted effort to
compensate for the vast expanses of nonrelatedness with expres-
sions of emotional availability and intimacy. They took a profound
look at the materialistic approach to life and decided that moder-
ation appeared more rewarding, more physically and emotionally
liberating.

A socially and professionally saturated life truly required some
technological support, such as a microwave. But to them, it became a
good symbol for their newly emerging form of relationship. Both the
socially saturated and the balanced and relaxed styles of life needed
to have intense heat — hard maintenance work — for the immediate
provision of physical and emotional nourishment. Monica and Mat-
thew truly loved each other, and their relationship blossomed because
individually they were able to fulfill their inner selves. They came into
each other's life out of fullness, not out of emptiness. They stayed to-
gether not as needy, dependent personalities, but as self-reliant and
mature mates who were able and willing to enrich their relationship.

Although we cannot pattern our lives according to other people's
styles and choices, each one of us has to face our own reality. It is a
fact that technology intensifies our emotional level. We choose to do
things that give us satisfaction. The media may convince us through
clever advertising that we need items to make us feel fulfilled. We need
to drive a certain car, vacation in an exotic resort, find love by wearing
the advertised perfume or the latest style of clothing, recapture our
youth by taking anti-aging vitamins, renew our energy by using a
certain type of physical fitness machine. The list can be endless, but
saturation sets in and dissatisfaction with life follows. Surely, some
of these things might give you a tinge of temporary satisfaction, but
will they give you inner contentment?

Tiny drops of water falling continually on a stone can wear a hole
in it. This old proverb illustrates how our daily living can wear down
our mind. Whether we engage in a monologue or dialogue, nagging
issues over appointments and disappointments, finances, illnesses,
toothaches, car repairs, travel, vacations, home improvements, in-
surances, deadlines, conflicts at work or at home — the list can fill a
chapter — saturate our minds and create mental overload.

If you are as imperfect as I am, you probably feel that this mental
saturation casts a shadow on your life, hindering your happiness.
Or you may believe that this is what life is all about, and there is

nothing that anyone can do to change it. Or you may believe that your situation is predestined or inherited because you were born into it and you cannot help but accept things as they are. If this is what you believe, then so be it. Stop reading this book.

Pause for a few minutes. For forty years in the healing profession, I have seen real transformation in the lives of many people. The opportunity is present in your life right now. If you have a hunch that your life needs adjustment or that changes must be made, the idea of restoring your self is definitely possible. I encourage you to reconsider at this point a couple of thoughts whose truths have survived for twenty-three centuries or more. One comes from Socrates: *No one is voluntarily evil.* You are not a bad person because bad things have occurred in your life. Besides, God the Creator of the universe did not create bad people. The other thought is from Plato: *Human beings are changing all the time—hair, flesh, bones, blood, and the whole body. It is true not only of the body, but also of the soul, whose habits, tempers, opinions, desires, pleasures, pains, fears, never remain the same in any one of us.*

Can you see the possibility of changing aspects of your life that are no longer desirable? Can you visualize your self removing certain obstacles from your path for growth and happiness? Accept the challenge.

One method that seems promising is the attainment of everything that we want—financial security, a good house, an expensive car, the ideal mate, and perfect physical condition. But sooner or later, desiring things will lead you to something that you want but cannot have. The alluring thought of wanting more does not work because there is no definition of what "more" is. More of what?

Brian, a brilliant and handsome lawyer, developed materially before he reached forty. He married a beautiful woman who was a psychologist, he built two houses, and he bought himself a huge boat. His loving wife drove a Mercedes, and he drove a Lincoln Continental. They belonged to an elegant country club, where they entertained friends and business associates. Yet they were not very happy. Underneath the beautiful surface of affluence was a kind of emotional unrest, leading to frustration, unnecessary quarrels, and reliance on alcohol. Brian admitted that a couple of martinis every night before dinner took the edge off his tension; an after-dinner drink became a ritual. As he attained more prestige and power, he sought emotional relief with a female colleague who worked in the same law firm. From an innocent friendship it became a passionate affair which led to a horrific divorce from his wife, who initially could not believe what was really happening. He married his colleague, and two years later he divorced her also and became interested in a younger woman.

Styles of life like Brian's propagate a perpetually pleasure-seeking society. Naturally, parents in such a society, to justify their own myopic behavior, indulge and coddle their children, making them as spoiled as themselves. An arrogant me-myself-and-I attitude ignores the fact that there are other people in this world who also have needs and feelings and who wish for a better life.

It is appalling to read in *Time* magazine, August 6, 2001, of a parent's attitude in the face of tragedy. Carla Wagner, seventeen, of Coral Gables, Florida, spent the afternoon drinking tequila, which she charged on her American Express Card before speeding off in her high-performance Audi-4. She was dialing her cellular phone when she ran over Helen Marie Witty, a sixteen-year-old honor student, who was out rollerblading. Charged with drunken driving and manslaughter, Carla was given a trial date — at which point, her parents asked the judge if it would be okay for Carla to go ahead and spend the summer in Paris, as she usually did.

Stories similar to those of Brian and Carla are not uncommon in our times. They indicate there is no guarantee that success and material wealth alone can give you the joy and fulfillment you are seeking. What seems to work more reliably is not pursuing everything that you want, but rather being content and appreciating whatever you already have available to your self.

You probably have heard or watched on television the tragedy of Christopher Reeve, the prominent actor who fell off a horse in 1995 and suffered a spinal injury, leaving him paralyzed from the neck down. In spite of his tragedy, he claimed to be a "lucky guy." In learning to deal with his feelings, he said, "I realized that the only way to go through life is to look at your assets, to see what you can still do; in my case, fortunately I didn't have any brain injury, so I still have a mind I can use."

Assessing his resources — modern medicine, a loving wife, and children — Christopher Reeve chose to use his mind to educate others about spinal cord injury and to write and direct film productions. He continues to live a productive and satisfying life.

For Your Consideration

~ You are reading this book. You may identify with certain parts of its contents and develop some feeling about what you have read thus far. This is normal. Books usually can give you solace in life, can help you develop ideas of your own, but they don't provide all the answers that you need.

~ The greatest of all books is life itself. Think about it. Your personal life is a book itself, and you are the author. There is a beginning and possibly a middle, but you don't know the end because you are still writing it. In essence, you are creating your destiny. Happiness or unhappiness is your own creation. No one else creates problems or miseries for you, not even God. Why should God be partial and make one person happy and another unhappy?

~ You cannot live your life without action. You have a brain and intelligence. Your own experience and wisdom tell you what action and direction to take. You are the way you are because you wanted to be the way you are. However, you have the power to become the way you want to be. You do have choices. In the beginning of this chapter you may have noticed that Monica and Matthew made some good choices, which proved productive. Unfortunately, we cannot say the same thing for Brian and Carla. Their choices were destructive.

~ Think of Christopher Reeve's story and don't let obstacles postpone the restoration process of your self. One thing that is very destructive in life is to weaken your own willpower. Your willpower says, "I can do it; I will do it; I have to do it!" If you stumble and fall once, try again; don't give up. Giving up is defeat. In accepting defeat, you will be crippling your creative energy.

~ Remember, no external means will ever help you to restore your self. These means have their limited sphere; they can only provide physical comfort. If you wish to have answers to life's adversities and regain inner joy, search within you and you will find real support and wisdom. It is there. All you need is to believe that it is there.

Chapter 10

DO EVENTS EVER CHANGE?

═══════════════════

The events in our lives happen in a sequence in time, but in their significance to ourselves they find their own order...the continuous thread of revelation. — EUDORA WELTY

ANY EVENT THAT takes place in a life is there to stay; it cannot change. Our attitude toward the event can change if we are willing to make the effort to adjust it.

Rita lost her mother when she was four. She may have repressed the grief or tried to forget her loss. As an adult, her life continues to be influenced by the experience she had as a child. She has a hard time getting close to people for fear she may lose them. She is not able to take in the love people are offering her because emotionally she is still standing at her mother's grave, refusing to let her go. Unconsciously, she is demanding a love from her mother that is no longer available.

You may have been deeply hurt by a friend. The hurt may turn into resentment that smolders within you and gets mixed up with the genuine love you have for the friend. You carry the resentment wherever you go and in whatever you do every hour of the day. You sit down to eat, and the memory of the hurt returns. You are about to go to bed, and the offender invades your sleep. Every waking moment you think of the hurt; you cannot let it go, so your hurt does not heal.

Derek, a social worker in his early thirties, wrestled with depressive feelings for a long time. He carried a nagging family secret which he was unable to reveal to anyone, not even to his therapist. In one of the sessions, his therapist, aware of Derek's resistance to move on with his life and frustrated over his constant complaining about the inadequacy of his mother, said, "Can you think of something good that your mother did for you?"

"Not a single thing; I hate her."

"Well, she changed your diapers, didn't she? Otherwise you would have died."

Eyes brimming with rage, Derek walked out, intending never to go back to therapy. But two weeks later, he called his therapist and made an appointment.

When he was six years old, Derek was hurt and sexually abused by a cousin who lived with his family, and later by an uncle who pretended to protect him and be his mentor. His parents, a quarrelsome and troubled couple, were oblivious to what was going on within their household. In their minds, Derek was an unhappy kid: "Growing pains; he'll be okay." Derek felt alone and abandoned; he especially yearned for his mother's care, but she was incapable of protecting him from his abusers.

He perceived his parents as two unloving people who stayed together because of the children, his younger sister and himself. His mother expected him to advance in life and possibly become a doctor like her brother. His father was a passive, rejecting male, unavailable to him for either emotional support or as a male role model. For Derek, there was no way to return to childhood to repair a relationship that had caused him emotional damage, a hurt that he carried into adulthood.

Derek had endured molestation and sexual abuse for seven years. When he dared to say he would tell on him, his cousin threatened to kill him. During his teen years, Derek was able to cope with his ordeal by detaching himself from his painful feelings, daydreaming that he was someone else and living a superficial life. Because of his high intelligence, he was placed in accelerated classes, but the structure of the classroom did not allow him to express himself, and he became a troublemaker. He failed to do his homework, he played hooky, he was disruptive in class, and he was defiant to his teachers.

College initially provided an escape from the horror of his home life. Eventually he gained some popularity — a much needed feeling of importance — by taking on school projects and planning events that pleased his professors. Some girls found him interesting, but he kept them at a distance. A superficial relationship with a troubled classmate seemed to interest him. He felt needed and tried to help her; then she wanted to marry him. Their short-lived romance faded away after graduation.

At the age of twenty-six, he worked in a hospital as a social worker, but he was still afraid of making friends, especially with women. E-mail and Internet were his main contacts with the outside world. Although he wanted very much to find a woman who could love him, marry him, settle down and have a family, he was terrified of meeting women. When he went on a date with a woman available for a relationship, he broke out in a sweat, talked about "sweet nothings," or spoke of grandiose ideas. If he promised her another date, he often cancelled it at the last hour. He gravitated toward older women who challenged him less, but then he found them less interesting and less suitable.

His work, which entailed dealing with people's problems, was boring; he was suspicious that he was being taken advantage of, and he loathed some of his associates. Evenings and weekends were spent at home overeating, mostly fast food, and he smoked incessantly. He admitted that occasionally he smoked marijuana, which relaxed him. When his thinking was clear, he admitted to himself that something was wrong with his life. A change was needed.

In therapy, he gradually came to understand one reality: his past could not change. Unlike a book or a film, it could not be selectively edited. It was there to stay, and its memory would evoke periodic pain. Reflecting on his situation — "No one understands what really has happened to me and how I feel" — the past held him prisoner. He realized that if he decided to be actively involved in the present, his pain would diffuse; he would be able to move forward and try his best to make his life healthier and more productive. Whether or not to be in charge of his current life was his decision.

Derek did not have to change, but his belief system did. His internalized thoughts about himself, not necessarily rational, were: "I'm insufficient, not acceptable to a woman with whom I might fall in love and who might be important in my life. If my own mother didn't care about me, how could another woman really love me? There is something wrong with me. I'm not okay. I'm unworthy and undeserving." These thoughts elicited fear, which could be understood as his initial terror, his infantile fear, and the perceived abandonment by his mother.

Two years later, Derek came to accept who he was. He was not insufficient. He was a good-looking man, intelligent, an avid reader of intellectual books, and capable of finding activities outside his home. A couple of women expressed interest in him, and he invited them out to dinner. Eventually he chose Kim, one of the two, and dated her for a whole year. During this time, he learned that in order to be loved and appreciated, he had to be appreciative, loving, and tender at the risk of being unhappy sometimes. When he began to feel that he wanted to be with Kim all the time and their intimacy became serious, Derek sought time out to think things over.

"Will she be good to me? Will she love me? What if she gets tired of me and rejects me?" These human questions and doubts needed consideration. Finally, Derek reached the point of answering his own questions: "If I am good to her, she will be good to me. If I love her and I am lovable, she will love me. If I respect and care for her, she will not reject me."

Kim noticed changes in Derek's behavior, yet her concern over his relentless smoking made her skeptical about his health. When she brought to his attention that she would not be happy with a smoker, after some debate he said, "This is my only bad habit." However, within a few months, he gave up smoking cigarettes and marijuana.

In a vigorous action, he began to sort out the many things he had accumulated in his apartment. What he did not need, he threw away or donated to the Salvation Army. He bought a treadmill and started his morning with a half-hour exercise. This physical action — clearing house and exercising — was symbolic of what he was doing on the mental level. Clearing out the old and useless and tuning up his muscles implied letting go of negative thoughts and getting the energy to move forward. In the process of getting his house in order, mentally and physically, he felt better.

Derek's style had been to charm women, use them to fill his own needs or to accomplish tasks for him at work. Ignoring the fact that his female associates were also human beings with equal rights and their own sacred souls, he manipulated them and took advantage of their kindness. Having a higher rank at his office, he expected them to be diligent and devoted workers. When a woman showed a tinge of interest in him or complied with his wishes, then his secret agenda surfaced: "I'd like to take this one in bed."

Assertiveness coupled with female intuition curbed his fantasies. Kim, a younger woman who had observed Derek's inclinations, challenged him into a realization that women were not subservient or objects to be exploited for personal satisfaction. They need to be appreciated, respected, and loved as much as men. She had a notion that under the facade, Derek was a good man; nevertheless, he had been a challenge. Marriage may change him, she thought. But change him into what? After the initial dates, she began to like him and sensed that he could honestly be a loving and caring man. She was delighted that he gave up smoking, a habit she detested.

Derek needed to restore his misguided self, to become his true self. He had to be liberated from his own victimizing thoughts. He had to stop attacking himself for not being good enough, for not being perfect. No one is perfect. We all have our flaws. It is natural to make mistakes, to feel insecure or ambivalent or scared. Accidents and traumas do occur in life. Most of the time we don't have control over them, yet to a great extent, we are in charge of our own lives.

In therapy, Derek was helped to approach his situation with care and compassion and to infuse himself with love. Mother was no longer around to provide the unconditional love that he needed when he was a child. Any changes that were necessary for his well-being now as a responsible adult, he needed to make himself. It was time to be in charge of his life. After a month's silence, time he needed for personal introspection, Derek finally connected with Kim and asked her to marry him. She accepted his proposal. Seven months later, they married and took a cruise to the Greek islands for their honeymoon.

I received a greeting card from them depicting the Acropolis with its crown of glory, the Parthenon. I have it on my desk for it brings to mind the story of Praxiteles, the sculptor, who carved the statue of Hermes with the infant Dionysius. A little boy named Diogenes came daily to the Acropolis to watch the sculptor at work. Patiently, the sculptor kept chipping away at a big block of white marble. After several months, Praxiteles had created a beautiful statue. In amazement Diogenes asked, "Master, how did you know that there were human bodies in that rock?"

"They have been there for thousands of years; I just knew they were there!" the Master replied.

Praxiteles knew that a perfect statue of a human body could be fashioned out of a huge block of marble. He had visualized the object of his creation. Convinced that it was there, he painstakingly chiseled away. As sculptors of our personality, we can visualize the true self that will gradually emerge from within. Kim and Derek visualized a potential in each other. They trusted their feelings, and with a responsible approach and a calculated risk, they entered married life. Of course during the early years of their marriage, and probably for the rest of their life together, they may have to do more sculpting. The chipping takes time, but it's important to remove obstacles, the wrongs, the negatives, and the destructive elements. How?

How did the sculptor do it? What sensory organ did he use when he envisioned the statue in the block of marble? It could be called the inner eye, creative intelligence, or spiritual awareness — all attributes of the soul. Whatever it was, it spoke eloquently of the human ability to create or restore. The story speaks to us about faculties about which we have not even dreamed; we know they exist within us.

Later in his life, Diogenes held a lighted lantern in broad daylight and searched for an honest man. I see his search as a human need to find the genuine part within that represents the authentic self. What does this all mean? In essence, we are searching for the core of inner being which will make our life meaningful, productive, and joyful.

While restoring your self, you will have better results and you will feel happier if you nurture qualities that are good and creative, such as understanding, acceptance, compassion, love, honesty, humility, peace, and joy. Instead of focusing on the *wrongs* of your personality, make an effort to enliven what good exists within you and consider its potential. Like Praxiteles, envision Hermes in the original big block of marble. Within you lies that healthy self that you will enjoy restoring and making whole.

For Your Consideration

~ Make a list of friends who nurture you, people who give you a sense of your own competency and potential. Surround yourself with them; in their nurturing company you will rediscover your true self.

~ Today, make a phone call to a friend who treats you as a good and bright person who can accomplish things. Speak to someone you can trust and in whose presence you feel comfortable. Encourage and cultivate feelings of friendship with that person by sharing experiences, planning an activity, or breaking bread together.

~ Take time out and spend it with your self. Be courteous, generous, and loving to the only self that you have. Each day of your life, leave enough time to do something that makes you happy, satisfied, even joyous.

~ Remember, you can be a genuine, loving, and caring person for others only if you are loving and caring of your self. No matter how unloved or unloving you have been, you can learn and relearn to love your self and others.

~ Learn to see your self as you really are, the true self, both at your worst and at your best. Then redefine your self as you experience it today by choosing the best part of you: less judgmental and critical, more gentle and compassionate, more tolerant and loving.

Chapter 11

FORGIVING AND HEALING

We are not meant to stay wounded. We are supposed to move through our conflicts, challenges, and tragedies and to help each other move through the many painful episodes of our lives. Remaining stuck in the power of our wounds, we block our own transformation. — CAROLINE MYSS

TEN WEEKS AGO, Justin left his wife, Melanie, and their three children aged eleven, six, and two to live alone in an apartment half an hour away from his home. He felt compelled to leave his family because of his involvement with another woman, Laura, an associate at work who was also married and was planning to divorce her husband. Justin developed a list of reasons to justify his departure from the family nest. As the saying goes, When you want to beat a dog, you can always find a stick.

Although Justin had seniority in his company, he felt insecure about his position. Hundreds of people had already been laid off; he might be next, he thought, and at the age of forty-four, he believed he was too old to start anew. His retired father was suffering from a stroke and needed his help. His eleven-year-old son needed expensive orthodontia, and his working wife divided her income between their hefty mortgage and the future college education of their children. These are not uncommon realities.

Justin had a hard time with critical family issues, and he felt worse each time he tried to discuss them with Melanie. Concerned with the well-being of her family, she too worked hard and felt overwhelmed by the behavior and progress of her three boys. In addition, she had to take care of an ailing mother. She noticed that her husband seemed under a lot of pressure. Most of the time he looked tired, restless, preoccupied, and emotionally unavailable. When she tried to be of comfort to him, his response was lukewarm. He did not want to share his feelings with her. "Why bother? She won't understand how I feel," he thought. In her own way she loved him and trusted him; she did not know that Justin found it more convenient and comforting to share his feelings during working hours with another woman.

The night before he left home, when Melanie complained about his diminishing interest in her and their lack of intimacy, he looked her straight in the eye and said, "I don't think I love you anymore."

"You don't? Why? I can't believe what I'm hearing."

"I don't want to be married to you. I can't stay in this house much longer."

"What's the matter? Haven't I been a good mother and faithful wife?"

"I'm sure you have. I've lost interest. I don't care."

"You don't care? What about the boys?"

"I'll pay child support and alimony. I want out. Can you understand?"

"I don't understand. Tell me, is there another woman?" Melanie asked, horrified.

"You're crazy. There is no other woman," he shouted, and he prepared to leave.

"Please, don't leave us," she pleaded.

"I'm not leaving the children, I'm leaving you."

"Then tell the boys what you plan to do." She controlled her tears.

Justin loved his sons, and the prospect of telling them about divorcing their mother and marrying another woman was distasteful to him. Silently, he looked at his wife and then turned on his heel and left his home. "How can I look my sons in the eyes and tell them the truth?" he wondered as he drove away.

Obsessed with his romantic involvement, he could hardly function. In the mornings, Justin dragged himself to the office, and by the end of the day he had accomplished nothing. He looked around at his associates and felt that everyone knew about his secret life. He bungled up a major job he had been working on and his company lost the contract. Enraged, his boss called him into his office.

"Justin, I have known you for ten years. You are a good worker, but the way you handled this project is totally inexcusable. One more mistake and you will join the unemployment line."

That night, Justin could not sleep. Confused and guilt-ridden, at four o'clock in the morning he called his wife.

"Melanie, I lied to you. We need to talk," he whimpered.

Shocked by the unexpected call at such an early hour, she said, "Talk? Talk about what? Is something wrong with you?"

"Yes, I want to tell you what a rotten bastard and betrayer I am, and I need your forgiveness or I'll kill myself."

Melanie's heart palpitated with mixed emotions. She did not answer. He had abandoned her, and the dreams she once had for their future together were shattered. Her nagging suspicion of infidelity devastated her. Could she ever again respect or trust Justin? Could she possibly expect comfort, safety, financial security, or companionship with him any longer?

After a few moments Melanie mustered enough courage to say, "I have been seeing a therapist every Wednesday for the last six weeks. If you really want to talk to me, let's meet in his office. Call him and make an appointment for both of us."

"Why don't we get together alone and talk?" he insisted. "I know I have done wrong, and I want to apologize."

"I don't think it's a good idea." Justin's infidelity was a bitter blow to Melanie, whose life's meaning was wrapped up in her family. When Justin asked for her forgiveness, Melanie realized that there was another woman, and instinctively she knew that his relationship with her was more than platonic. She made up her mind not to forgive what she thought to be an unforgivable betrayal. Although deep down she knew that she loved her husband, she felt wounded and indignant. She consulted her therapist, and he suggested that she and Justin meet in his office to talk about the situation.

In the therapist's office, Melanie cried. "I've heard of people having affairs, but I never thought you would. You deceived me, Justin, and I hate you. I can no longer trust you. A manipulative liar, that's what you are. What would the boys say if I told them that you committed adultery?"

"I cannot tell you how sorry I am. I don't know what got into me to be so stupid. Melanie, I beg you to forgive me..."

"I'm not God," she interrupted.

"Please! I know I did something terribly wrong. I have committed adultery, and I can only blame myself for being insensitive and stupid. I'll never forgive myself for hurting you like this. I did an evil act, but I'm not an evil person."

"Why don't you tell the therapist about your affair?" Melanie said in an angry voice.

Guilt-ridden and despondent, Justin admitted the details of his pas-

sionate affair with his associate for the past three years. He felt caught
in the web of a serious conflict, torn between his family and a busi-
ness associate, a gorgeous woman who eagerly listened to him and
stimulated his creativity. Guilt mounted day by day as he left the pres-
ence of his lover and returned to his home, or as he left home to go
to his lover. By the end of the third year, he decided that his family
was more important than the affair, which had become increasingly
demanding. Laura was determined that Justin was the man of her
dreams. She wanted to marry him and have a family of her own.
He was not about to start another family, and he did not know how
to tell her that he could not go through with their initial plans. Al-
though convinced that he loved her genuinely and did not want to
hurt her feelings, under the circumstances both sets of feelings had to
be sacrificed. Justin decided to return to his wife. He realized that he
could not deprive his children of their father much longer, and that
he could not give up years of history with his family.

Remorsefully, he again asked Melanie for forgiveness. He promised
to be faithful and do whatever was necessary to restore their relation-
ship. She looked at him with compassion and said to the therapist,
"I want to believe that he's sorry, but how can I trust him? How do
I know this won't happen again?"

"It won't happen again, ever. Please believe me," Justin said, eyes
filled with tears.

Melanie folded her arms across her chest. Tears of anguish, angry
feelings, bitterness, rage, hate, culminated in an urge to attack, hurt
Justin, and retaliate. As hostility subsided, their two tormented souls
floated in a sea of venom, sinking in confusion and pain.

"Both of you are hurting," the therapist said, "and I wonder if you
can tell me what it is that you need?"

"Can you help me kill the demon in me?" Justin said with a
bittersweet smile.

"We need help to face reality," Melanie added.

"I want to return to my home. I love my wife and I love our sons."

In subsequent sessions, both realized that each of them had con-
tributed toward the deterioration of their marriage, perhaps not in
equal proportions. Self-blame provided a way to rebuild their mar-
riage. Both believed that if they could change — be more caring and
attentive to each other's needs — they might be able to cope with
an unforgivable injury. As they began to realize the areas of their
married life in which they fell short, they felt they could still be in

charge of their lives and make the adjustments necessary to restore their marriage. It took several individual sessions for Melanie and Justin to bring peace and joy back into their lives. Before any actual marital therapy began, each partner had to do serious individual self-restoration.

After the anger and its dangerous consequences were adequately explored and understood by the betrayed wife, forgiveness, the ability to let go of the violation, became the focal point of her therapy.

Forgiveness proved to be a major issue for Melanie. When feelings of anger took over, she was full of resentment and felt unable to forgive or to let go of her husband's betrayal and allow healing to take its course. Of course, since she was hurt, anger was a normal human reaction. Nonetheless, she had a choice to decide to forgive what she considered an unforgivable offense or not to forgive and feel resentful. At the end of one session, the therapist gave her a clipping from an article that appeared in his e-mail. "Read this," he said, "and we'll talk about it at our next meeting." He presented her with the article:

Do You Resent Somebody?

Resentment is a result of repressed anger. If we are not able to forgive someone who has hurt us, if we cannot let go of the hurt, a permeating resentment takes over our whole being and controls our destiny. The moment we begin resenting a person, we become his slave. He controls our dreams, absorbs our digestion, robs us of our peace of mind and good will, and takes away the pleasure of our work and our life. He ruins our religious beliefs and nullifies our prayers. We cannot take a vacation without his going along! He destroys our freedom of mind and hounds us wherever we go. There is no way to escape the person we resent. He is with us when we are awake; he invades our privacy when we sleep. He is close beside us when we eat, when we drive our car, when we are on the job, or when we are with a loved one. We can have neither efficiency nor happiness. He influences even the tone of our voice. He requires us to take medicine for indigestion, headaches, and loss of energy. He even steals our last moment of consciousness before we fall asleep. So, if we want to be slaves, we can harbor our resentments.

The following week, Melanie said to her therapist, "I read the clipping twice and pasted it on my mirror. It makes a lot of sense. I guess I'll have to forgive the rat," she said with a smile.

"The 'rat,' or the imperfect human being, your husband, who failed you?" the therapist said.

"Forgiveness is easier said than done," she said, "but I'll try."

It appeared that she had made a decision to forgive Justin. She also needed to forgive herself for the way she had felt about him since the time he had abandoned her.

The act of forgiveness can be a decision and a fact, but the feeling of forgiveness may come only in time. When we confront unforgiving feelings and the permeating resentment that they evoke, we need to deal with them honestly, own them, accept them as our inner turmoil, and work through them constructively. We need to be in control of how we feel, and we need to be in charge of how we act and handle our feelings.

In time, Melanie developed an inner strength as she let go of the traumatic event in her marriage. She stopped the endless "Whys?" and made a conscious effort not to mention or discuss her husband's affair anymore. Slowly, she internalized the concept of forgiveness, a positive aspect in her life that gave her relief. However, as her attitude toward Justin improved, he drifted into a deeper state of depression. Her reassurance that she forgave him caused profound guilt feelings in Justin. "How could I do such a horrible thing to my wife whom I really love? Why did I get into such a mess? Shame!" Justin could hear his own voice echoing in his brain. Feeling miserable for failing, he refused to forgive himself. It was symptomatic that on the week she forgave him, he had two car accidents. In the second accident, he totaled his car. Unconsciously, he was punishing his thoughtless self. Self-punishment after the marital violation seemed to play a major part in his depression.

Justin's depression was not of physical origin. A psychiatric evaluation indicated that his depressive feelings were not the result of chemical imbalance, which could be treated with antidepressant medicine.

His depression was most likely the result of personal loss or failure. Justin understood it as a result of the violation of his family. He felt guilty, and guilt immobilized his life. He felt tired; he experienced lack of energy and incentive. These obstacles were hard to overcome. His therapist asked about other possible reasons for his depression, such as repression of negative feelings — unpleasant memories of past wrongs, childhood traumas, current conflicts, and disturbing thoughts. Justin's recollections were poignant, tearful accounts of events that he had repressed. His mother was killed in a car accident before he was five; his father remarried, leaving Justin at the mercy of an uncaring stepmother. His father's job entailed frequent travel for long periods of time. His stepmother mistreated Justin, locking him out of the house hungry or slapping him frequently for not meeting her expectations. In school, diagnosed as being learning disabled, he felt isolated from his peers. Both home and school experiences left Justin with pronounced feelings of rejection and failure.

Later in his married life, when Melanie became a mother and her attention, by nature's design, shifted from Justin to the children, again he felt left out. Sensitive to feelings of rejection from the past, he felt rejected once again, this time from the woman he loved so much. It was then that he began to drift away from his marriage, unconsciously seeking a mother's love. Feeling angry and miserable about his life in general, he pursued companionship and solace from another woman.

The gradual realization that he could not change the past offered him a new challenge. The task ahead was to accept unconditionally the traumatic events of his earlier life, to forgive his supposed offenders, and to face the present realistically. In the presence of his wife, he was always aware of his offense. He had hurt his wife, and although she forgave him, he could not forgive himself. It took many therapeutic sessions for Justin to mature through the pain of failure, to take seriously Melanie's and God's forgiveness, and to apply it to himself. In essence, Justin had to tell himself, "God has forgiven me; my wife has forgiven me; and it's time for me to forgive my self."

For Your Consideration

~ When a spouse decides to forgive the other for a serious offense, the partner must allow negative feelings to subside and warm feelings to return. Even when you forgive an offender, resentful feelings that may still be present need to be acknowledged and resolved. You may need to return to your self; apply your own good qualities for your personal healing.

~ Forgiving the person who hurt you and forgetting what that person did are quite different, although you may think the two are the same. Even if your forgiveness is genuine, forgetting does not follow immediately, if ever. Wounds may heal but scars often remain. Remembering the offense is normal, but forgiving could be a healthier choice, inviting the offender back to a former and even better relationship.

~ You may be able to forgive others and yet have a hard time forgiving your self. For many people, self-forgiveness is difficult and self-punishment continues. "How could I have done such a thing?" Be honest with your self. Can you really forgive anyone if you cannot forgive your self?

~ The source of many mental conflicts is the refusal to forgive self. If you are suffering emotionally or mentally, consider forgiving your self for being human, and therefore imperfect. Healing, inner peace, and joy in your life are impossible, unless you begin to experience self-forgiveness.

~ Self-forgiveness does not mean condoning or absolving your self of the responsibilities and consequences of your wrong actions. Self-forgiveness points out offenses and failures. It does not mean self-pity or self-judgment. It means repentance, accountability, and change. It also means facing the harsh reality of your actions and the decision to restore the damaged areas in your life.

Chapter 12

SENSITIVE AREAS

The true heroes of life are not the triumphant victors but the defeated who find a ray of hope. — ELISABETH LUKAS

DOES TIME HEAL all wounds? Sometimes it does, leaving a sensitive scar as a reminder while life continues its course. Memory, however, does not always allow a total cure for the wounded. In some situations, time does not heal all wounds; it provides, instead, opportunities for paving the way to healthier days.

The death of a child opens the deepest and most painful wound in the hearts of parents. It causes the ultimate pain that a human being can endure. Regardless of how many children are in a family, the loss of a child leaves an emptiness, an incurable wound with the surviving parent to grapple with questions like: "Why did it happen?" "Why me?" "Did I do something wrong to deserve it?" "How can I live through it." The only beacon of light that brings relief is often the memory of joyful days that the deceased child brought to the family during the time that he or she was alive.

Steve, my former classmate and friend of fifty years, lost two daughters, Maria and Elaine, whose death plunged him into profound depression. Condolences and comforting words from relatives and friends did not relieve his pain. Medication did not help, and antidepressants made his condition worse, for his body was chemically intolerant. On the first anniversary of Elaine's death, Steve again experienced the whole syndrome of depressive feelings: loss of interest in life, loss of appetite, loss of patience, and sleeping difficulties. He could no longer work or pursue his hobbies: gardening and building model airplanes. A major accomplishment of which he was very proud was an airplane he had built from scratch; he had flown it in different parts of the country. He lost interest in it and sold it.

In a recent conversation, I asked Steve how he felt about his life.

In a tone of sadness he replied, "Above all, I believe that Maria and Elaine are still with me, and one day I will be with them. Their deaths have been an indescribable loss for me. Nothing can fill the gap they have left in my life. They, in their own ways, were remarkable women — kind, considerate, and idealistic. Parents love their children. It is a blessing when parents also like their children. I loved Maria and Elaine. I also liked and admired them. For me, the adage "Time heals all wounds" is not true. Time is merely a veil obscuring the initial pain that occurs with death and loss. That veil parts many times and brings the pain fully back. I see a child that reminds me of my daughters when they were young. I hear a voice like theirs. So many things. Yet somehow I have come to understand that it is also a blessing when the veil parts, because I relive those moments, and I am reminded of the ways my daughters enriched my life and how fortunate I am to have had them in my life. So I struggle through depression. Most of the time it passes and my life goes on, and I see the goodness of things again."

In full empathy, I can only imagine Steve's struggle, a journey beset by fogs he did not see coming. Asking why these painful or, in some cases, wonderful events in our lives occur is a waste of energy. We can never know totally all that was involved in creating these moments in our lives and why they happened. In psychological terms, we need to get past the question "Why" and focus on healing, because the event has already taken place and it is not going to change. At best, we can allow the gentle glow, the healing power within each person, to suffuse every part of body and mind.

Steve, a gifted and loving human being who for most of his life offered comfort and joy to many, still struggles to find comfort in his own faith. He may pray to a God he is not sure he believes in, but his choices are limited. The advice he used to give to those he had comforted and helped was, "God hears every prayer, regardless of whether or not we believe in Him at the moment we pray." The God of compassion and love wants to know the depth of our pain, the darkness we experience when tragedy occurs. Prayer may be another source of help, a real "gut-level prayer" for comfort, which connects the suffering person with the Healer of all pain. Such prayer recurs throughout the psalms: "Out of the depths of my heart I cry to You, O Lord, hear my prayer!"

Adversity comes in all shapes and sizes. Perhaps your adversity is less dramatic than that of my friend Steve, yet more personal — a lingering trauma in your past, an undiagnosed illness, a relationship break down, or a nagging doubt that threatens to shake your faith. Should doubt enter your mind, take it to God in prayer. Let God touch, absorb, and heal your knotted spirit. In such states, your trust in God is tested but it is also in a state that your faith truly expands, as you will notice in the following story.

Father Frank is a Greek Orthodox priest, one of the most likable, energetic, and productive men I have ever met. Married — Orthodox clergy are allowed to marry, but only once — he is a family man with a wife and five children. He has been in the ministry for forty-five years. Known for his initiatives and innovative ideas in education, he is admired by his colleagues and considered by the hierarchy as one of the most accomplished clergymen in the Orthodox Church in our time.

Referring to him with his permission, I intend not to praise his virtues and unprecedented accomplishments, of which there are too many to enumerate, but to share his sheer pain over the many personal tragedies that he has had to bear as a human being. Recently, while I was taking him to the airport, he summarized his feelings by relating the following vignette:

"I was at the cemetery, dressed in my vestments and ready to offer a prayer over the graves of my two sons. I focused on the two tombstones and reread the inscriptions. Stanley died at seventeen; Nicholas died at thirty-three on the eve of his third wedding anniversary, leaving his wife with a two-year-old daughter. On my right stood my grief-stricken wife, Anastasia, struggling to control her tears. In a wheelchair next to her was my daughter Nikki, a victim of multiple sclerosis, lately abandoned by her husband after twenty-two years of marriage.

"As I offered prayers for my sons' eternal rest and for the health of the rest of my family, spontaneously my eyes were raised toward the sky, and I asked, 'Why all this, dear Lord?' It hurts as I think of my losses. Yet the cross of Christ is of great comfort to me. If He endured the pain of the cross, who am I to complain?"

"Your faith must keep you going," I said.

He grinned and said, "Well, being a Christian is like being pregnant: either you are or you are not. Either you have faith or you don't. My faith nourishes me daily. God knows my situation; He gives me the needed strength to combat it. I believe in a God of love who is in charge of our lives. He has created all things and sustains the universe with utmost power and wisdom. Therefore, He has a plan for each one of us. Someday we will know why all these tragedies occur."

"I admire your faith," I said.

"That's the only thing that sustains me. As a believer in God's grace, I am not meant to remain wounded. I am determined to move on through my tragedies and challenges and to help others move through the many painful episodes of their lives. That's how I perceive my destiny."

I have known this priest well for forty years and have been present in his life through all of them. Today if you met him, a gifted and loving man, he would give you the impression that he is happy. If you need his help, he will do anything to serve you, offering comfort or infusing you with his genuine love. Blessed with a good disposition, he cracks a joke at an opportune moment to make you laugh, or he walks that extra mile to be of service to you.

To me, Father Frank's life remains a mystery. Truly, life is a mystery. How he has endured the ultimate pain that a human can experience, the loss of his two sons and the affliction of his only daughter, and still continue an inviolate ministry as a priest is a mystery. He no longer spends time asking why these painful events occurred in his life. He focuses on the healing of his soul in every unfolding moment and on the welfare of his family. He looks for meaning behind each of his losses and finds comfort and healing power as he recollects happy memories in his sons' short lives and in the legacy of love transcending death.

Often he visits the cemetery and meditates. He claims, "The sight of my sons' tombstones brings back vivid memories of their last hours, when I witnessed their pain and their deaths. I recall the emotional anguish and helplessness that my wife and I felt. But with each visit as I relive these events I question the Lord. In what way was He present? What was His part in my life when my world was collapsing? Of course, as a loving God, He had to be present. He knew that my feelings of resentment, anger, and bitterness had turned me against Him. He knew what was in my heart then; why should I hide it?

"In expressing my true feelings to Him — at times bitter and harsh words — I knew that He would not reject me. Honesty has helped me to clear the air, cleanse my soul, and feel closer to my Lord. I trusted His unconditional love for me, even when my attitude was angry, arrogant, and weak. Our human weaknesses are sparks that fall into the ocean. Does the ocean catch fire? The ocean is His love."

Father Frank spends time talking and interacting with his four grandchildren, whom he loves dearly. He derives comfort, hope, and joy from his daily life. He believes that healing takes place in spurts. He invests time and energy in being creative and in sharing the joys and sorrows of his congregation.

It is my personal conclusion that this piece of clay, because of his unshakable faith, was able to forgive and love the God who allowed these tragedies in his life, even when he felt let down and disappointed that God permitted so much pain. He was able to forgive himself for the angry and negative feelings he had experienced both as a priest of God and as a human being when the uninvited intruder, death, visited his family.

Of course each one of us cannot perceive life as this priest does. He has faith that God will carry him through his pain. For most of us it is not always easy to maintain a strong faith. In fact, there are those who make fun of faith, likening it to superstition. However, the truth is that faith is good for the health of our physical and emotional being. Medical study after study show that patients of faith recover from illnesses more quickly and live longer than people who lack faith. Those who practice their faith find themselves stronger and more resourceful in critical moments. As we go through a traumatic or tragic time, we tend to look at every new experience through the lens of the wound. It is virtually impossible not to be influenced by a personal emotional injury. If you are emotionally wounded at this time of your life, or if you feel that you are more wounded than someone else, you may consider the challenge of healing and restoring your self as you interact with other people whose presence may be refreshing.

At times of great sadness and personal crisis, we feel more tender-hearted and closer to our inner self. When we are most confused and buffeted by the vagaries of life, when nothing external can comfort us, we thirst intensely for spiritual guidance and wisdom that the twin within, our spirit, can provide. Difficulties and disappointments often help us find and strengthen our inner self, our soul. If we could only listen to it. The joys and sorrows of our lives are also presenting us with tremendous opportunities to rediscover who we truly are. Life has a lot to offer us, if we are willing to be humble recipients.

The requirements for healing are stringent, especially if they demand that we come to terms with our tragedies. Events do not change. No medication or comforting words can change the hurtful events in our lives. Dwelling on a wound — Why me? What have I done to deserve this pain? — is self-flagellation that hinders healing. You may or may not have suffered a tragic event. But once such an event takes place, it cannot be undone. It is time to stop the bleeding and pursue areas of life that need attention. When you plan to remodel your house and you start tearing down walls and piling debris in a dumpster, you are careful not to throw away anything that is valuable. You pick up the valuable parts to use them in your new building. This principle applies as you are about to remodel your self.

Restoration of your self would be better served if you investigate your past for positive patterns as well as for negative ones. You need to bring out the strong and enduring parts of your personality and leave behind the negative patterns that may damage your life. "What will I do with the negative thoughts that I harbor?" you may ask. Ask the next question, "What purpose does negativity serve in my life?" Your answer to these questions may reveal a new direction. Delving into your self and focusing on the positive parts is essential to your restoring process. You must have done something good in your life. Think about it. Your good thoughts can powerfully influence your feelings about your self and your behavior.

Restoration of your self requires internal as well as external change. It requires that you ask your self a few questions:

~ Who am I?

~ What's my purpose in life?

~ Am I fulfilled by the life that I am leading?

~ Am I giving enough attention to my needs?

~ What are my ambitions and goals?

~ What are my aspirations and plans?

~ Am I trying to please everyone in the hope of gaining their love?

~ What are my expectations of others?

~ What realistic changes can I expect to make in my life?

These questions one by one need to be answered with sensitivity, determination, and an action plan. Why not make a new beginning with your self-restoration at this very moment?

For Your Consideration

~ Release your fears, anxieties, and defenses that cluster around the sensitive and hurting part of your inner self. Do not preclude feelings of pain. You cannot pretend that you are not hurting. Reach within your self and touch gently the parts that hurt. Bring a new message to your heart and tell her with courage that life needs to continue in spite of the pain. Be benevolently present and say something soothing to your self. You are not seeking a cure; you are looking for healing.

~ Do not run away from your present reality. Adversity is a reality that none of us can avoid. As you meet your difficulties with courage and faith, you will emerge on the other side stronger, with renewed hope and commitment to life. Turn around and face your adversary and transform it into an ally that ennobles you. Don't ask, "Why?" Simply ask, "How can I best respond to what is happening to me now?"

~ In situations where scientific knowledge fails to offer comfort, human sensitivity must take over to soothe the pain with empathic words. Facing inevitable pain, believing there is no meaning in anything, we walk on thin ice. A minor shift in attitude brings us to firmer ground. "To thine own self be true" — with what a promise Shakespear's phrase sings in our ears!

~ In time of crisis, instead of succumbing to despair, consider three options: faith and belief in God; acceptance of empathy and understanding from caring people; pursuit of meaning in your present life. Remember, no suffering can defeat us if we are prepared to search for its meaning; no loss is conceivable that does not hold the possibility of at least one meaning — that is the answer we owe to ourselves.

~ You are not alone in the world. You are surrounded by people, and some of them are loving. Your own well-being cannot be the main purpose of your life. Well-being in a vacuum, separated from interpersonal relationships, is nothing. In God's benevolent plan everything works out well. Important lessons derive from our own choices and our losses. Discover your purpose and clarify your belief about the continuity of life and its ultimate destination.

~ PART FOUR ~

SELF-ACCEPTANCE

Being out of touch with just how wonderful we are causes double trouble. It keeps us from truth; it keeps us from joy. If we don't accept ourselves as we are and tend to assault ourselves with unrealistic expectations, we are deprived of the most important thing in the history of the universe, our life. If we accept, love, and enjoy ourselves, we become free and live life to its fullest.

Chapter 13

SOMETHING IS NOT QUITE RIGHT

Rejecting ourselves does not change us, it actually multiplies our problems. Acceptance causes us to face reality and then begin to deal with it. We cannot deal with anything as long as we are refusing to accept it or deny its reality. — JOYCE MEYER

AS WE STRUGGLE with the multiple issues of daily living, it is easy to feel frustrated and even angry. "Something is not quite right," we say. As anger seeps into our being, we can easily lose sensitivity and compassion for ourselves. This state of mind can lead to a feeling that we are useless and worthless. We may look at people around us, especially at those who seem successful, and think of ourselves as failures or victims of life's injustices.

Although it is part of our nature to compare ourselves with others, with those who seemingly have it all, it is unfair to label ourselves as the "have nots."

Why? Because comparisons breed insecurity and envy. We find ourselves missing something significant. As we invest energy in brooding on our ill fate, we feel deprived, emotionally paralyzed, and impotent.

Stephanie, a thirty-six-year-old artist, sat in her suite and gazed through her window, puffing one cigarette after another and thinking, "Life is hopeless; I'm a failure. I'll probably never find a man to marry, never have children. Nobody cares." After a five-year relationship, her fiance of the same age decided that he was not ready for a lifetime commitment; he needed to date other women before he settled down. Heartbroken, she consulted authorities, read books, asked friends, and attended lectures to find answers, which none of them could possibly provide.

Fantasies and daydreams about the past and future, fantasies about a new career, an ideal job with a six-digit salary, maybe travel, romance, and luxurious living — surely some of these would come her way. Such thoughts held her inactive and impotent. Unrealistic ex-

106

pectations tarnished her appreciation of life and weighed down what she had available to her self: a loving mother, a caring brother, some good friends, physical health, intelligence, and skill. She had a college degree in commercial art and could find placement, but no job was good enough.

Don't we all tend to think of the ideal mainly in terms of the fulfillment of our desires and the security of our place in the world?

Some psychologists claim that seven basic needs seem to control our lives. These are:

1. **Security:** We would like to have both financial and emotional security. How wonderful it would be to have enough money to buy things that we need for a comfortable and luxurious life. The question is, once we have all that we want, does that guarantee security? In reality, people who apparently have everything in abundance are abundantly insecure. A constant sense of insecurity in knowing how to maintain or increase their possessions permeates their lives, and the insecurity is compounded by fear of losing what they have. Besides death, one thing that is secure in our life is our insecurity. But the voice of our true self reminds us: "Seek spiritual riches within. What you are — a human being with an eternal soul — is much greater than anyone or anything else you have ever yearned for." If you turn off the yearning, you are never going to feel totally secure. No human being does. Accept your insecurity as part of your human condition.

2. **Recognition:** One of the problems in life is our desire to feel important. We want someone significant to recognize our importance. It is not a bad desire, and it feels good to be recognized, but it is not always attainable. It starts early in life when parents validate the presence of a child in their life. The child feels good to be accepted, praised, and recognized as an important member of the family. Some children who do not feel important in their home in spite of their good behavior get recognition at school for bad behavior. Schoolteachers can attest to this reality. In the adult world, besides being gainfully employed, we seek to be recognized for our emotional fulfillment.

3. **Love:** Love is the oxygen of the soul. As well as needing parental love for our early survival as children, throughout life we need to be loved by at least one other person. Without it, we perish

emotionally; we die prematurely. But in order to receive love, we have to be a good recipient of love and lovable. Mature love is a state of being in which the satisfaction or security of another person becomes as important as one's own. It is a strength within that enables us to give power, freedom, and peace to another person. In a state of love there is respect, concern, and affection for the other person and not simply mutual exploitation or mutual satisfaction of needs. As in mature sexual behavior, one does not give and the other get, but both give and receive at the same time. Can you envision possibilities?

4. **Adventure:** A well-planned adventure can provide another dimension to your life. It could be a trip to an unfamiliar country, a cruise to the Caribbean Islands, a ride in a hot-air balloon, parachute jumping out of an airplane, rafting down a tumultuous river, traveling around the world. In the spirit of adventure, some individuals undertake a measurable risk in financial investments or in a commercial enterprise.

5. **Creativity:** Creativity is the Creator's will within. The Creator of the universe has made us His co-creators. Most humans carry the spirit of creativity within them, but they do not always express it. The daring ones explore whatever talent they have to its fullest and get results. The timid are afraid to employ their innate gift. Your life is the most precious art. You don't have to be a famous artist or renowned author or a talented poet. Simply, roll up your sleeves and do something that you like. Allow your intuition to guide you. To live a creative life, you must be willing to let go of the fear that you may fail.

6. **Belonging:** Humans were not created to live alone. It is a most profound need to belong to a loving family, to a caring person, to a productive organization. Nature teaches us a vivid lesson: Sturdy and tall trees have the deepest roots. If human beings are to grow and develop their potential, they need strong roots, a good family support system. Belonging to a loving spouse provides intimacy, tenderness, and security. Belonging to a church or a temple where you actively participate gives you an opportunity to cultivate your personal spirituality. Furthermore, it links you to other people — the *koinonia* or community of believers — where sharing experiences can be very rewarding.

7. **Worthiness:** All of God's creation is worthy of admiration. While every part of God's creation and every creature has its own purpose and its own value, a human being stands out in its importance and worthiness. Judeo-Christian theology considers a human being as the crown of all creation. In biblical language, God created Paradise, a place of bliss for our progenitors, Adam and Eve. God wanted them to be happy, because He loved them. When humanity deteriorated and suffered corruption, God sent His Son to redeem and save the world. God became man so man could become Godlike. All this points out the worthiness of a human being. Apply this concept to your self. You are God's creation, endowed with intelligence, energy, and freedom. There is a place for you on this planet. In God's eyes, you are a worthy person. As your body, mind, and spirit coexist, their harmony can provide for you happier days.

The above needs, and perhaps some that you might add to the list, are neither good nor bad. They are part of our human nature. But how we perceive these needs and how we go about fulfilling them can bring joy or misery to our lives. The way we choose to go makes the difference.

Every day we are faced with numerous decisions and choices. You are holding this book. You have a choice to read it or put it down and watch television. Only you can decide what you want to do. Often we don't choose the thing that we know is good for us. Granted that the *right choice* may be a difficult one, and it might involve some sacrifice of pleasure. Surely it is much easier to look at something on the screen than it is to involve your mind with reading. Yet the choice is yours as to what is of lasting benefit to you.

Making the right choice tends to be a challenge, and oftentimes you may not be sure what the right choice is. It helps when you take time to understand where you are at the moment, where you want to go, and then actively engage your mind in what you need to do. By making choices in your thinking, you can willfully direct your actions.

As Stephanie discovered, sitting alone and indulging in escapes is not the answer. The secret of self-restoration lies in rediscovering who in the world you are and mobilizing your energy and courage to be that person, to be authentic. The richest and most lasting joy is a result of knowing your self intimately. The old adage "Know thyself" is the first step. Appreciate who you are, cherish and develop your good qualities, chisel off the bad ones, activate your ability, and make choices moment by moment that demonstrate that you accept who you are.

You may have picked up this book for a reason. Perhaps you are looking for a solution to a nagging problem or you may be experiencing some of the following symptoms:

~ I'm angry about my life. I expected it to be different.

~ I feel bored with my surroundings. My friends seem indifferent.

~ I'm frustrated with my job, but I don't know what else I can do.

~ Often I feel depressed. Antidepressants don't seem to help.

~ At home, my mate is expecting too much from me.

~ My parents are too demanding of my time.

~ Wherever I go, I experience a sense of not belonging.

~ I find myself sitting and watching television, flipping channels and finding nothing of interest.

~ Most of the time I feel lonely.

~ Something is missing in my life, and I don't know what it is.

~ I don't think anyone really cares how I feel.

Do any of the above symptoms apply to you? If your answer is yes, don't lose heart. One of these or a combination of all or of most of them is part of our human nature. Personally, I have dealt with most of the above problems and other adversities. In the process, I learned quite a bit about who I am and what I need to do. As a result, I wrote this book to indicate that there is a way out. Once you start considering the contents of this book, I can reassure you, many wonderful things can happen in your life. "In my life?" you may ask with a tinge of skepticism.

Yes, in your life. But do your self one more favor: be attentive to the following sentences. Currently, your state of mind may be troubled; you have a conflict, and you are unable to find a solution. Your physical and emotional health may be suffering; your living conditions may be deplorable. You may be grieving over a major loss in your life. A doctor may have given you a scary report on your health. Your father may be undergoing chemotherapy. You have just received a phone call that your best friend is dying.

Many are the evils that occur in the world, and most of us experience our share. We don't always get what we think we want, and that makes most us feel unhappy some of the time. Born into this life, somehow we are to experience both physical and emotional pain. Birth, growing up, aging, illness, loss, grieving, as well as disappointments happen to every single human being. This is not all terrible. We can learn something from each problem. Difficult issues teach us to have a realistic attitude toward life.

Most of us live a programmed life. Controlled by our psychological patterns, we are hostages to unconscious drives, needs, and impulses. We stay in jobs we hate; we repeatedly choose relationships that are hurtful. We don't know how to break habits that are self-defeating; we don't know how to correct distorted perceptions; we don't know how to find better, more creatively satisfying ways of being. That's unconscious behavior. In reality, no human being wakes up one morning and says, "I'm going to feel bad today." The old proverb "No one is willingly bad" is just as true today as it was at the time of Socrates who first said it.

As we go through difficulties, we rediscover our tremendous potential for solving problems. Everything is workable, and there is fulfillment and joy as we work on solutions rather than burning time on problems. You probably have had your own trials and tribulations. When a painful episode occurs in your life, you may be seeking reasons for your suffering. It is important that you don't blame anyone for your pain. Do not assume that God is punishing you for some wrong you have done. If God were to punish us for our sins, the population of this planet would have been extinct a long time ago. Don't blame God, your parents, or anyone else for your condition. Just take responsible action. Even at this point, you may be facing a serious problem without solution in sight. But complaining or wallowing in despair will not be of any relief to you. At this unique moment, why not consider an alternative? Make it easy on your self.

For Your Consideration

~ Every problem — be it with relationships, finances, health, or self-image — has a solution. By going within and meeting your friend, the self, you will see that external fulfillments, however important, do not provide an adequate solution. The solution is already available within and can be accessed without the assistance of external forces.

~ When your personal life becomes difficult or hazy, who is going to help you? Only your own friend within, your inner self who will say, "I am here; why are you afraid?" Accept and befriend this unseen part of your self. Once you become aware and confident that you have a friend within, you will never feel lonely.

~ Every human being has to seek its own way to make the self fully alive, more noble, and more productive. A secure way in seeking restoration of the self is total acceptance. You have to accept your self, knowing that whatever behaviors you exhibited in the past, even the destructive ones, left you with great lessons to follow.

~ Without being defensive, yet with self-confidence say, "I am what I am." You do not need to conform with the majority, imitate others, or agree with them in order to keep their possible favors. These others have their own style of life, which cannot influence you unless you allow it. Be true to your self, to your intimate others, to faith in God, and inner joy will follow.

~ Leave negative thoughts and self-defeating habits behind you; do not waste energy trying to outthink or manipulate or reform them. Think of your self as a spiritual being and develop thoughts and habits that are of benefit to you. Allow your self to believe that you have a soul, and this part of you is divine. Not only do you have a soul, you are a soul that abides in a human body.

Chapter 14

THIS IS WHO YOU ARE TODAY

Perfectionism doesn't make you perfect: It makes you feel inadequate. You are not worthless because you can't do it all. You are human. You can't escape that reality, and you can't expect to. Self-acceptance is the goal. — MARIA SHRIVER

TAKE A PEN AND PAPER, sit down, take three deep breaths, and relax. Now, write on small index cards the word "Self-acceptance" in large print and place them in prominent places where you can see them during the course of the day.

This is who you are today. Your yesterdays, regardless of how bad or good they were, can only serve as lessons, but they cannot change. You have neither control over the events of your past nor can you change them. Nobody can. Life is not a book or a film that can be selectively edited. In spite of what your life is today, accepting it and adjusting to it will give you healthier days and the capability for a new direction.

Self-acceptance will create new space in your life so that you can move with ease. Your ability to feel closer to your self will make it possible to accept your self for who you are. Self-acceptance will help you to replace thoughtless reactions with thoughtful responses. It will easily let go of anger and consuming resentments, and will invite understanding, compassion, and love, making your life more peaceful and rewarding for you. It will restore a glow to your face that will radiate to others, making you an attractive companion.

If you have emotional wounds that have not healed yet, or if you are still faced with an incurable situation, consciously or unconsciously you may want to protect your self. An immediate defense mechanism is to distance your self from your feelings, the wounded part of your self. Too much pain propels you to walk away from your self and shut the door behind. "What's so bad about that?" you may

113

ask. Walking away from your emotional self will make it difficult to accept your self.

Chances are that you are facing a situation that seems beyond your control. You wonder how you will handle it. You spoke to your parents or to a close relative or to an intimate friend, you prayed about it, but your situation remained unaltered. How do you handle a shattered dream, a painful disappointment? How do you redirect the yearnings that fill and overflow your emotional world?

The following five ways are what most people choose in troubled situations:

1. **Avoidance:** Running away in an effort to protect our selves from further pain may work for a short time. If a leak in a big boat is not corrected, that boat will eventually sink.

2. **Denial:** We tell our selves that there is no problem, that we shouldn't sweat over small things. Although we feel the discomfort for a while, we allow things to get worse, and the emotional toll on ourselves is destructive.

3. **Giving up:** When we give up or quit, the emotions that follow cast a shadow around our being and we feel inferior, inadequate, impotent. We ignore the hope that, accompanied by patience, may relieve our despair.

4. **Projection:** Unable to resolve our situation, we tend to blame others for our "bad luck" or misfortune. Some people blame their parents, especially their mother; others blame God. They project on them feelings that are personal. What seems to work to our benefit in times of trouble is for us to take responsible action.

5. **Conformity:** In a state of despair, rather than follow what we believe is true and good for us, we conform to the opinions of other people. In the process of listening to external authorities, our initiative and creativity are drained, and we sink into depression.

Restoring your self implies that you open the door and welcome the wounded self, as one would welcome a warrior who survived the battle. Come closer to your self in order to rediscover who you really are. While getting deeper into your self, you may recognize the mental blocks that hinder your vitality and energy. Being in touch, observing, and accepting your self is essential for inner growth and personal contentment.

As you take a personal inventory, what areas of your inner self are you observing? To pose the question plainly: "What is the truth about you?" The most important discovery that you can ever make is the truth about who you really are. You are more than you know — more than your physical self, more than your intellectual or emotional self. You are a spiritual being.

"Me, a spiritual being?"

Yes, you! You are God's wonderful creation. Your birth into this world was not an accident. Your parents may have caused your conception, but your birth as a human being is God's miracle. You are in this world for a purpose. And once you establish what your purpose is, life is going to have greater meaning for you. No matter what you believe about your self at this moment, you have within you even greater potential for health, love, creativity, wisdom, freedom, abundance, and joy. This is your true self.

Now comes the next question: "Do you like your self?" You are aware that many people do not like their true selves. There is a self-rejecting attitude that causes turbulence in the mind, and this attitude escalates in our daily encounters with others.

Suppose you start treating yourself as someone important, as you would treat a dear friend who came from afar to visit. "I'm glad you came," you might say to your friend, and you try to make the visit pleasurable. If you would do this for a friend, why not befriend your self and start liking who you are in spite of your shortcomings. You may not like certain things that you see in yourself, but that is not a reason to hate yourself.

Rejecting your self does not help you feel better. It actually multiplies your problems. Feeling insecure and unworthy may keep you from seeking people who are good-natured and nurturing. Instead, you may seek the company of people who are aloof and rejecting — thus proving to your self that you are worthless and undeserving of acceptance, kindness, and love.

Instead, why not develop the kind of mature attitude that says, "I can like who I am and accept my self so I can move on with my life. I know that I will not always remain this way. Any improvements I need I will make gradually. I want to change. And as of this moment, I sense that a change is occurring within me. Can I really change? What will I do? Where will I go? Will it be different?"

Science reminds us that almost every cell in our body changes every seven years. We know that ongoing change — of body, mind, and spirit — is part of our life. You don't have the same body you had ten years ago. Your thoughts about life and living are not the same as they were three or five years ago or even six months ago. Your spirit or disposition may be different today. Think of how you felt about an issue or an idea a year ago or a month ago.

Every morning you wake up to another day, and you can create it according to what thoughts and feelings surface in your mind. You can say like the Psalmist, "This is the day that the Lord has made, I shall rejoice and be glad in it" — and believe this affirmation. You can apply your inner strength or you can continue to relive the same daily drama: "Oh, what's the use! Who cares?"

Acceptance of your self enables you to face reality and then begin to deal with it. You are not able to deal with anything as long as you refuse to accept it or deny its reality. This effort offers you an opportunity to accept your self as you are. Remember the words of an old and popular song: "I love you just the way you are!"

People who reject themselves do so because they cannot see themselves as proper and right. They focus on their flaws and weaknesses and ignore their beauty, their strength, and their potential. This is an unbalanced perception, a result of what other authorities may have instilled in us. Perhaps their critical eyes focus on what is wrong and weak rather on what is right and strong. Inevitably, we internalized the image or identity that our parents or significant others gave us when we were children. We wanted their love and approval, so we accepted their definition of us. But as we grew older, we discovered other qualities about our evolving selves that made the difference. In essence, we said, "This is who I am," and we redefined our real selves.

For Your Consideration

~ Insecurity and feelings of unworthiness will keep you from being able to receive things graciously. You may feel that you must earn or deserve whatever comes your way. You may even become suspicious: "Why am I getting a present?"

~ Rejecting ourselves does not change anything in our life. It actually multiplies our problems. Acceptance causes us to face reality and deal bravely with real issues.

~ Surround yourself with people who respect you, who are fun to be with, and who treat you as a human being. In their presence, you will feel physically comfortable, emotionally nurtured, and well accepted. Then, you can reciprocate by becoming a friend.

~ Stop listening to external voices that tell you what you should do. They might cause confusion in your life. Nobody really knows what is good and beneficial for you. Start trusting your self and try to hear that silent voice within you that says, "This might work, give it a chance."

~ Take a risk! If what you have tried in the past has not worked, risk something different. Taking a risk builds self-confidence, not because you always get what you go after, but because you mature through new experiences. If your risk proves to be a mistake, it is not the end of the world. A mistake can be a good lesson.

Chapter 15

BECOMING WHO
YOU WANT TO BE

<hr>

Whatever God's dream about man may be, it seems certain it cannot come true unless man cooperates.

— STELLA TERRIL MANN

YOUR SELF-EVALUATION has introduced a new image. While you are the same person, your inner self has a greater awareness of who you really are. "This is who I am," you say, and in the same breath you may raise two more important questions: "Do I have a chance?" "Has anyone ever succeeded in this earthly enterprise that we call human life?" Beyond any doubt, the answer is *yes*.

Some men and women do enjoy a quality of living in spite of adversities. These are real people who stand out with particular warmth and brilliance. They have eyes to see, ears to hear, and a heart to love. They are generous, peaceful, undisturbed even in their misfortunes. You may not see their names in a newspaper or their faces on television. These people are seldom the popular heroes. They are much too happy to seek external approval or official attention. How have they attained such an admired position?

In reverse, we can ask the same question of other people, the failures, the misfits, the vandals, the thieves, the criminals: Were they born that way? Did the environment form their character? Did they work toward their own deterioration?

A large number of the so-called modern heroes are an artificial product of mass media, encouraged and supported by our perceptions and dire need to be entertained. Most of them, including some gifted multimillionaires, are often very far from leading happy lives. What is missing?

Sid Cheney, president and CEO of a successful firm, has asked me several times: "What is missing in my life? Why can I not be happy?" He achieved success and acquired many things that would make others envious — a loving wife, healthy children, a beach house for summer vacation, opportunities to travel, a membership in an exclusive country club, and many friends.

As he talked to me about his daily life and his aspirations, it became evident to him that it was not happiness that he lacked. His family, material acquisitions, and his professional achievements provided a great deal of happiness. What he did not have was inner joy. He lacked that deep, inner feeling of lasting joy, trying to be the person he was meant to be.

Sid had to give up the struggle of competition and the search for more glory, more success. He no longer needed to impress his colleagues or his friends. He realized that the secret to a joyful life was an attitude of gratitude for what he already had available to his own self and his willingness to be authentic, honest, genuine to the person he really was.

This could be the best invitation for you: *to be who you really are.*

For a few precious moments, let's consider what your life is like and how you spend your time. Examine your choices, your current condition, and where you are now. Tune in and listen. Open your soul's ear, the inner ear of true listening, and see if you can hear, feel, sense, and know for your self, with certainty, what compels and calls you. Can you distinguish your own true calling? Your main objective in this reading is not just to make a peaceful living, but to make a rewarding life.

Ask yourself: How do I spend my days? Do I sit around waiting for a miracle, daydreaming that I might be discovered or hoping to win the pick six lottery? For the most part, am I doing what I generally like or am I just "doing time"? Is my work-life mostly composed of chores and compromises, duties, responsibilities and obligations? Or am I passionately engaged in following the dictates of my inner self? What would I do differently if I could? Would I change jobs if the current one was unrewarding? Would I abandon a long-term relationship that was abusive and without direction? Would I get into a program to lose weight so I could feel better? Would I confront my boss and tell him that I'm underpaid for the quality of work I do? All these question have answers. The issue is to choose the most direct route to your highest, deepest joy and well-being.

As you apply your own unique combination of special gifts, talents, experiences, and interests, choose a basically honest, meaningful, and helpful approach for your self and others. The approach needs to be harmless, fulfilling, realistic, and psychologically and socially rewarding.

If a job is your concern, it has to be fulfilling financially so that you may provide sufficient support for your loved ones and for your self. Ideally, your job could be contributing to a brighter, happier, safer world and better society. Finding meaning and purpose through work is a major part of rediscovering who you are and what you are here to do. It is important not to miss out on this element of truth in your life. When you are dissatisfied, sometimes you find that truth by changing direction and looking for work that is more satisfying. During this writing, I met a lawyer friend I had not seen for years. Richard, in his early forties, decided to change career.

"I no longer practice law," he said with a smile.

"Have you retired?" I asked naively, thinking that he might have made enough money to take it easy.

"I opened a restaurant, and I'm very happy about this change." His exuberance was evident in his facial expression. Could Richard really have changed direction without much thought and without hearing that inner voice?

Sometime in our lives the only thing we can reasonably do is try to find more satisfaction in the work that we already have. Personally, I have certainly had this kind of experience. I love my work: I like to say that I have found appreciation, freedom, peace, and joy by being a psychotherapist, a family man, and a writer. I'm grateful.

If you find your self killing time and procrastinating, hoping for a better time or opportunity to attain what you want out of life, ask yourself, "What is really holding me back?" I pray that reading this book will help you to find the answer.

A year ago, I worked with a woman who serves as a good example of what it means to refuse to be held back. Liz, a talented woman who for seven years worked for a publisher, became very dissatisfied with her daily routine. The corporate world that once excited her now stressed her out. Income and benefits were substantially good, but the increasing expectations of the publishing firm caused frequent migraines. At thirty-three, with a husband and a five-year-old child, she became more aware of and uneasy about her emotional needs. She thought her self as a spiritual person, and she wanted to be a loving wife and a good mother. Her prestigious job and salary were excellent, but she did not feel fulfilled. Money was plentiful, but the happiness of her family was her priority. She sensed great fulfillment in being a mother and wife, yet something was missing.

"I feel bored and confined. There are other things that I could be doing," she said to her husband, who was concerned about her unhappiness. A solid and well-established businessman, he encouraged Liz to pursue her dreams; whatever she wanted to do, he promised to be supportive.

In college, Liz had majored in mass media communication and had made several educational films for her church. Journalism excited her, and she had written several inspirational screenplays that gained her significant recognition. She perceived her self as a humanitarian, and being dedicated to her family, she wanted to produce psycho-spiritual films for television. Such an ambition required persistence and hard work, and Liz was willing to make the effort. She quit her job and began to tap her resources, the Internet and personal contacts with interested people. The response was overwhelming; she realized that there were great opportunities out there where she could use her talents. The challenge — "How and where do I start?" — caused confusion and ambivalent feelings which resulted in procrastination. "I need time to process my thoughts," she said.

Time she had, but in view of her many interests, she needed to focus and to appropriate time for each aspect of her aspirations. Liz began to devote part of her time to the fulfillment of each project. She felt happier when she had access to her qualities and strengths, shifting identification from one to another. She made herself a schedule, which she followed faithfully. For example, the days and hours that her son was in kindergarten she appropriated for writing screenplays. Late evenings, when husband and son were in bed, she did some film-editing in her basement. Weekends were strictly spent with her husband and son, forging the image of a happy family woman.

Liz could not have been happier when she completed her pilot film for an educational channel. This opened new opportunities for the fulfillment of her dreams. She was offered her own weekly TV show.

Through her writing and educational films, she gained recognition by her church, which employed her part-time to develop a promotional missionary documentary film. She was able to assemble parts of different films made by people who had spent time in Africa, and she made a new version, *The Dancing Church*. This effort received much acclaim by other denominations, and it brought her a substantial amount of money and a great deal of personal joy.

Liz allowed herself to let go of her former job, which offered financial security. At the risk of making less money or none at all, she took a chance to explore her capabilities. Eventually she developed into a prolific writer and creative film producer. This fulfillment of her dreams, applying what she believed she could do, gave her impetus and courage to become an integrated person, a better wife and mother.

For Your Consideration

~ We might be aiming for the stars, but we cannot reach them. Let's be realistic and not beat ourselves up with the superhuman delusion. Superman and superwoman are illusions meant to excite our senses and lead us into a fantasy world. We admire the rich and famous, movie celebrities, accomplished athletes, authors, and artists — they appear elegant and happy. Yet does anyone know what their real life is like, and how they feel off the stage? Can you or I really live an exciting, successful, wealthy, super life as proclaimed in magazines and television?

~ When we compare ourselves with others, usually we seek individuals who seem to us better, more gifted, more talented, more of everything. We wish to be like someone who looks great. At least that's our perception. Then we feel bad because we don't even come close to resembling that person. Simply, we cannot be like anybody else. We can only be who we are, and that is okay. Why not bank on our own assets, capabilities, talents, and gifts that God gave us?

~ Remind your self as you travel down the road that you are your own person, a worthy human being, and you can do some good things for your self and others. If some people in your path treat you thoughtlessly or try to tear you down or block your growth with negative thinking, try to understand that they are projecting their own mental conditions onto you. Avoid them, for they can ruin your life. As Eleanor Roosevelt said: "No one can make you feel inferior without your consent."

~ In her book *The Artist's Way* Julia Cameron calls such negative people "crazymakers." Cameron claims that often crazymakers are charismatic, inventive, persuasive, and destructive.

"Whether they appear as your overbearing mother, your manic boss, your needy friend, or your stubborn spouse, the crazy-makers in your life share certain destructive patterns that make them poisonous playmates."

~ Next time you catch your self saying or thinking, "She is driving me crazy," ask your self why you are sabotaging your own happiness by being in that person's presence. Your life is very important to you. But it is like a puzzle. Figure out where the pieces go and put them together yourself. Other people might give you well-intentioned instructions. Remember, nobody — except your self — has the right to choreograph your life.

Chapter 16

SELF-ESTEEM

Feelings of self-esteem can only flourish in an atmosphere where individual differences are appreciated, mistakes are tolerated, communication is open, and rules are flexible — the kind of an environment that is found in a nurturing family.

— VIRGINIA SATIR

Do you ever have moments of intense anxiety? Do you often feel irritable? Do you ignite easily with outbursts of uncontrolled emotions? Do you find yourself carrying an ongoing anger? Do you lack motivation? Do you alienate yourself from people and circumstances when things do not go your way? Does excessive guilt permeate your life? Does a new direction ever appeal to you?

If your answer to any of the above questions is yes or a qualified maybe, your self-esteem may be low, causing you disturbing symptoms. Of course medication may relieve you temporarily of your symptoms, or a sympathetic therapist might help you to reconstruct your life. However, only you know your needs, and you have to decide what course of action to take.

You may have already started the process of regaining your self-esteem by reading this book. Now, stop for a moment, breathe slowly and deeply, think carefully and say, "I'm able, capable, and willing to keep going. The Holy Spirit within me will provide direction." That was not difficult, was it? Repeat these affirmations once more. Perhaps you already feel better, sensing an inner change. It is a new beginning for you; accept it. It can be filled with anticipation and promising challenges.

From now on, each conscious or unconscious step that you take will send you over the edge into the unknown. Because of your increasing knowledge about your self, your responses to this may be different. You may find the challenge appealing. With inner confidence, you may see the untried areas as opportunities to expand your skills and knowledge, to discover more about your environment, and to notice that you have real potential.

If you are a timid person, you will view the unfamiliar aspects of life as dangerous areas to be avoided. If you fear failure, you will doubt your ability to deal with something new and exciting. "Nothing succeeds like success; nothing fails like failure" prove to be true axioms in human history. Suppose you have tried something and failed again and again; realize that you may have a fresh start at any moment you choose. This thing called "failure" is not the falling down, but the staying down.

An experience or a project that has failed does not make you a failure. In many areas of life you may not be competent, but there are a few things that you do really well. The most important thing is not to beat up on yourself. It is a no-win situation if, no matter what you accomplish, you tell yourself it's not good enough. Stop setting yourself up to feel inadequate. Decide what appears realistically "good" to you in each endeavor and go for it. Pursue obtainable goals that will keep you moving and maturing.

Avoid the trap of comparing yourself to others. Comparing how bad you feel on the inside with how great someone else looks on the outside is a losing proposition. You will always come up short. No dog would do to itself what you are doing to yourself. A little dachshund does not go around thinking it is inferior because it does not have the long legs of a greyhound. Greyhounds do not put themselves down by saying, "I'm a failure. I would have made it if I had been short and cuddly and could sit on someone's lap." It takes a rational mind to do this hatchet job on oneself. No apple wishes it were a banana, and no banana suffers a feeling of inferiority because it is not like an apple; the apples are not sitting around wishing they were as big as watermelons. They are fine the way they are — and so are you. You are whole and complete and capable just as you are. You may not be a banana, but you are a fine and sweet apple or pear. Being a fine apple or pear is enough. If you do not feel that you are enough, you will give out signals of inadequacy, dependency, and "Oh, poor me." Your friends, mates, or associates may feel sorry for you for a while, but they won't be available to you much longer. When you label yourself with a negative adjective, you are disabling yourself. The only possible reason you do not feel okay is that you are telling yourself you ought to be different. Different? In what way? Being someone else? Would that make you happy? Isn't that an illusion? Why not make a different choice? Introduce your self to the beautiful, capable, and lovable you and let others discover this you. Virginia Satir, a renowned therapist, invites you to repeat her creed: "In all the world, there is no one else exactly like me. There are persons who have some parts like me, but no one adds up exactly like me. Therefore, everything that comes out of me is authentically mine because I alone chose it."

Imagine that your employer gives you a problem to solve, and this type of problem is not part of your job description. Your boss wants you to take over a new project. You have not been presented with the background material necessary to understand the project, let alone complete it in a set period of time. However, eager to please your employer, you agree to accept the assignment. Then you torture your self, convinced you should have asked for more information; you have no idea how to perform the task. After agonizing over the situation, you make a decision that turns out to be unfortunate, with harmful consequences. Guilt rushes in because you feel you should have made a different judgment — although you know you could not have approached the job differently because of your lack of knowledge at the time of your decision. In all manner of situations and in crises and disasters where people can do nothing but stand by helplessly, self-esteem suffers needlessly and unjustly.

Many people make totally unrealistic demands on themselves. Unable to fulfill them, they flagellate themselves with self-criticism, using as a whip a standard of perfection incompatible with their own abilities or with normal human nature. Absolute perfection even in inanimate things is a rarity. In humans, it is unattainable. When Jesus exhorts us to seek the perfection of the Father, what He means is that we should never be content to emulate what passes among us for perfection, goodness, wisdom, purity, or love. We should stretch ourselves to the limit. Humans, however, are not omniscient or omnipotent or infallible.

It is self-defeating to compare yourself unfavorably to others. As often as not, such comparisons lack the basis of full knowledge: that exceptional someone is accomplished — you are a klutz; she is poised and self-assured — you are a miserable nail-chewer or a handkerchief-wringer. But when you get close to Mr. or Ms. Perfect, his or her warts show.

Certainly there are heroes and heroines both small and larger than life. There are fine outstanding people you meet and know, as well as great men and women in the world arena. It is well to admire them, even envy them, but do not measure your self unfairly against them and their attainments. You cannot know their private anxieties and insecurities. The limelight in which the great ones live and the aura you tend to see around the familiar faces hide a great deal. You and I are fallible and mortal. Although there is absolutely nothing wrong with admiring and wishing to emulate people who are manifestly good examples, it is wrong and needlessly damaging to denigrate your self, your individual, unique, precious self.

Each person is significant simply because each of us is alive. You may be less or more significant than many others on the scale by which the world measures importance. Nevertheless, as an individual responsible for you own thoughts and feelings and actions — that is, for your own life — your worth is equal to that of every other living person. You possess precisely the same measure of control over your life as does the greatest world figure. The sense of uniqueness and worth comes with every new model as original equipment. None of us is born with the feeling of unworthiness. Like a taste for oysters or Limburger cheese, the feeling of unworthiness is acquired during the course of development from childhood to adulthood.

You may derive a great deal of comfort and strength if you take time to reexamine your attitude toward your self and understand its hidden origins, come to terms with your yesterdays, and confirm what you are worth today. You may be surprised by your own value as a person.

Family members and other significant adults do influence even the most independent lives, contributing directly to happiness or unhappiness, fulfillment or the lack of it. The alienation that characterizes many families invariably can be traced to the low self-esteem of one or more of its members, inherited from a previous generation.

Timorous persons fear failure so much that they take no risks, and so fear conquers them. Without at least an occasional *leap of faith,* low self-esteem can only go lower, and the inner decline in one's sense of worth brings emotional atrophy and pain. Retreat or surrender becomes progressively inevitable; your sense of personal efficacy especially in crises diminishes while the feeling of powerlessness increases and eventually overwhelms you.

Obviously this principle applies equally to all areas of life. If you remain silent and unprotesting when ideals you count important are under assault — silent because you are afraid of not being accepted —

then you are, in fact, acquiescing under the attack. When you retreat from life's challenges and opportunities and burrow into the safety of the familiar and the undemanding because you are afraid of failing at something untried, then you have guaranteed your failure.

People often prefer to blind themselves to a serious defect in their marriage partner rather than face it; they fear damaging the relationship. More likely, they fear having their own worst flaws brought to light. In all situations of this nature, such fear, elaborately veiled, camouflaged, and rationalized, tends to breed insecurity, timidity, and a further loss of self-esteem.

There are people who are driven compulsively to pursue meaningless sexual adventures, one affair after another. Fear of loneliness drives them from relationship to relationship. They fear being regarded as unattractive, and so they have to prove their attractiveness over and over again to their pathetic selves.

We frequently confuse self-esteem with pride. Although the two are related, there are significant qualitative differences. Self-esteem is founded on the conviction of one's fundamental efficacy and value as a person. Pride is the pleasure one derives from achieving a certain goal or successfully meeting a challenge. Put another way, self-esteem is the inner confidence one has that one can do a given task. Pride is the pleasurable consequence of having done it. Self-esteem says, "I can do it. Pride says, I did it."

Beyond these dynamics, however, there can be profound moral differences between the two. It is not by accident that pride appears on the list of the seven deadly sins. It has earned its place. True pride in one's achievements and attainments is neither wrong nor unattractive as a character trait as long as it is founded on and is derived from a healthy and sound self. Overwhelming pride that betrays an unwholesome and distorted self is deadly. We all know the obnoxious person whose whole attitude proclaims, "I'm the best employee in the office. I have money in the bank. I have a flawless family."

If, in spite of your best efforts, you fail in a particular project, you may not experience the pride that would have come with success, but you will experience a real sense of pride in knowing you did your best. If you are secure and rational, your self-esteem will not be diminished. On the contrary, it may be enhanced. In other words, your self-worth need not be contingent upon your particular successes or failures, for the outcomes are not always under your exclusive control. It's the "how you play the game" adage. Yet failure to understand this causes much needless anguish. If you persist in judging your self by norms and factors that you cannot control or norms that are not realistic, you place your self-esteem in constant jeopardy.

All learned behavior can be unlearned. If you have been conditioned to feel unworthy, you can be reconditioned to accept your full humanity and know its full value. Whether assisted or guided by your own lights or by professional help, you have the capacity to investigate and understand the root causes of your tendency toward self-deprecation. Having accomplished this by applying all the better parts of your self, all your energies, you can reeducate your self to develop a positive and constructive view of your self.

There is quite literally no earthly force that can stop you from restoring a marred and flawed self-image, provided you desire to restore it. From the moment you consciously reject the tarnished image of your self that parents, teachers, or peers have foisted on you and consciously determine to focus all your intelligence and your emotional and physical resources on the objective of renewing your self to its original God-given state, renewal has already begun.

Who has not observed those fortunate people who are equipped and prepared to meet life in full confidence and independence? It shows in everything they say and do. They seem to pour themselves out onto life as though they were pouring water onto parched earth. Their resources seem miraculously without limit, as indeed they are. They act as though they had no fear of ever running dry, as surely they never will. To them, the world is obviously a lovely place to be. They feel distress when they find things as they ought not to be, but they strive to alleviate their distress by alleviating the unacceptable condition. As in the proverb: "They do not curse the darkness but light a candle." Blocked in one direction, confident people simply try another direction and usually have fun whichever way they take.

Persons wanting in self-esteem, unsure of their resources, are forever "counting their pennies." Nothing comes easily to them. Everything seems to provide cause for complaint. Where others see the bottle as half full, to them it is half empty. Demanding all from life, they are insensitive and unresponsive to its demands on them. They envy those around them and withhold their inferior selves from people as much as possible. When they fail, others are to blame for the failures. When they succeed, they rob themselves of the joy because they are convinced it is less than their due. They are grudge-collectors who always have a complaint, even against God. Persons with a healthy sense of self minimize life's dangers, its bad deals, its failed promises, and move on with courage and determination to seek other opportunities.

As their self-esteem rises, they demonstrate outstanding qualities: they have a strong sense of family and are able to relate effectively with people. They have a high moral and ethical sensitivity. They manage to stay away from alcohol and chemical substances. Regardless of the type of work they do for a living, they are productive. They like to make money, but their lives do not revolve around financial matters. Their perception of success is viewed in terms of interpersonal relationships, not in terms of material possessions. They are charitable and contribute generously to worthwhile causes.

Life can be fascinating, endlessly rewarding, often beautiful. It would be silly to deny that it can also be, and often is, boring and inconvenient and ugly, with periods of drudgery and penalties and sheer grossness. But it is axiomatic that the way you view this world depends on how you regard your self. Beauty — like happiness and security and hope and goodness — is, ultimately, in the eye of the beholder.

By ignoring or letting go of our self-esteem, we die a slow emotional death. We cease to have courage and determination to face life as it unfolds daily in front of us — unannounced events that we encounter. Today, the human race faces problems that have brought us all to the edge of despair and catastrophe.

Since September 11, 2001, when the United States suffered a barbaric act of terrorism, the whole world has been shaken with fear and uncertainty about the future. Yesterday, we felt strong and invincible; we were the most powerful nation in the world, and our fears were only hypothetical. We were vaguely concerned with disasters that had not yet happened. War was an evil that occurred far away in foreign lands. Today, war is taking place in our land, and our fears are real. The catastrophe that took place has left us feeling vulnerable, and we wonder what catastrophe will follow. Currently, young and old are profoundly disturbed by the anthrax attack. We are worried about future biochemical attacks by the terrorists and the possibility of the use of nuclear weapons by those who do not value human life. Our home life, our country, the whole world will be in danger of destruction if the present trends continue. But what a big "if" this is. Humans are not likely to remain passive in dangerous situations.

Evil seems to triumph only for a while, but it is always defeated. Our leaders will not stand still waiting for another attack. We need to trust their ability and good judgment to defend our country and protect us. However, our first responsibility will be to return to our inner self, the unseen part of us, and remodel it to its greatest potential.

An old Chinese proverb puts things in perspective:

> If there be righteousness in the heart, there will be beauty in the character.
> If there is beauty in the character, there will be harmony in the home.
> If there is harmony in the home, there will be order in the nation.
> When there is order in the nation, there will be peace in the world.

We have already witnessed the human potential in the midst of an incredible disaster. The restoration process started immediately. Most people, activated by the spirit within, reached out to help. While the police force, firefighters, doctors, and professionals in the art of healing were making heroic efforts, putting their lives at risk to rescue lives, our whole nation began to face upwards toward Almighty God. Grief-stricken hearts and minds, united in fervent prayer, sought refuge, strength, and comfort in God.

Shaken but not broken, we proclaim that we are "one nation under God." Along with the overwhelming humanitarian efforts to restore the image of our country, to comfort the afflicted, and to restore our personal image is the desire to come closer to God. As humans, where else can we go?

Self-esteem, then, or *pride in being a human being,* is one of the greatest needs facing the human race today. Our survival and security depend on hope, faith in God, and love for one another. Hope, faith, and love can truly stimulate and sustain self-esteem. These three virtues, rightly perceived and proclaimed, become the healing path to a more spiritual life, as we will discover in the following four chapters.

For Your Consideration

~ Healthy attitudes — using our heads, our hearts, and our hands, no matter what we do for a living — will help to increase our self-esteem and to nurture our spiritual life. In making an effort to help others, we discover how good we can be. We can sense a joyful feeling when we evoke a smile in another person by an act of kindness.

~ The workplace provides a rich arena for us to become more aware of our actions and intentions, as well as to help us take concrete steps along the spiritual path. Working our selves the way we work at our jobs with respect and dedication can be self-transforming.

~ On some level, every work situation will present us with obstacles: control, frustration, power plays, pride, lies, apathy, jealousy. Be careful not to overreact or to be overpowered by any of these emotions; they are part of our human nature. Do not let them possess your mind and obscure your clear thinking.

~ Avoid the tendency to pass judgment on others' thoughts or behavior. Try to see good in others. Self-examination is good; it helps to chisel off bad habits. Yet if you are too judgmental of your self, what purpose would that serve in your life today? Perhaps you can be a little more alert about your attitude.

~ Maintaining and increasing your self-esteem suggests an effort to develop your spiritual self. The path to spirituality is not a smooth, straight, ascending road to happiness. When you start combating barriers, your own personal shortcomings, life can get more difficult before it becomes more coherent and tranquil. A great deal depends on what aspects of life you have been ignoring. Certain things will inevitably surface as you get to know and accept your self. Your patience, persistence, and perseverance can be rewarding. During this time of your life, reading a good book or talking to a spiritual friend or to an experienced religious person can be of great support.

~ PART FIVE ~

SELF-
TRANSFORMATION

From childhood to adulthood and to old age we go through many physical transformations. At the same time, something special and good is growing inside us. We need to give it proper sunshine and nourishment to ensure that it grows to health and vigor. Meanwhile, we live in a state of tension between two realities:

a. *the world that endangers our existence tempting us with hopes of happiness and demanding our obedience to its laws, and*

b. *the supernatural existence of God for Whom, even unknowingly, we yearn. This Divine Being calls us forth beyond the laws and boundaries of our life to the service of a spiritual life that starts here on earth and continues in God's Eternal Kingdom.*

Chapter 17

TRANSITIONS

Curing implies the end of trouble; you don't have to worry about whatever was bothering you any longer. But caring has an ongoing attention. Conflicts may never be fully resolved. Your character will never change radically, although it may go through some interesting transformation.

— THOMAS MOORE

UNLIKE A VALUABLE PIECE of furniture or a precious painting that can be completely restored within a certain time frame and remain intact, the restoration of self requires a long time, persistent effort, and constant maintenance. As long as you are alive, there will always be something that you can do to improve and refine the self. As we have explored in previous chapters, the complexities of our human condition do create obstacles to our growth that need to be removed and problems that need to be identified and resolved.

However, resolution involves an inner discipline, a gradual process of identifying and rooting out destructive patterns and replacing them with new and constructive behaviors. To regain and sustain a healthy self requires the development of resources that can facilitate and nurture the restoration process. With a caring attitude, you need to ask your self: What is it that I want out of my life? What steps do I need to take to attain a healthy and satisfying life? Then allow a little time to hear the answer from your own self.

Contemporary civilization provides abundant means for our physical convenience and enjoyment. Medical science provides effective medications and sophisticated surgical procedures for our optimal physical health. Psychiatry and psychology offer medication and techniques for healing and stabilizing our mental health.

Although we live in a world of wonders that offers astonishing options for our well-being, the saturated self asks: Where do I fall short? Why am I so unhappy? In spite of what I have, I am not satisfied. Then comes the next question: *What is really missing?*

If you are asking such questions, it is essential that you reconsider and recognize the importance of your inner transitions — that is, how everyday experiences enhance or hinder your perceptions about life and living. You may call this recognition a conscious effort to explore and develop the unseen part of you, your spiritual self.

This process can be pursued in two ways:

a. You can start from where you are in terms of your own personal religious orientation or belief system. Different religions serve the spiritual needs of different people. According to your cultural background and religion, you may consider embarking upon a spiritual path that is best suited to your present state of mind and natural inclination.

The purpose of this chapter is neither to convert you to any particular belief system nor to analyze, criticize, or evaluate any religion. All major religions can make an effective contribution for the benefit and spiritual stability of humanity. Whether divinely inspired or not, they are all designed to make our world a better place and the individual a happier person. However, one common requirement is that if any religion is to have some impact upon an individual, it needs to be sincerely practiced not with intellectual prowess or verbal eloquence but with sincere disposition. To serve the objective of this chapter, we can show respect for diversity in religions and appreciation for the spiritual nourishment that they offer to their followers.

b. You may explore familiar yet basic human qualities, such as acceptance of other human beings, caring, compassion, forgiveness, goodness, generosity, kindness, love, respect — all of which, to some extent, are already your own property. This exploration is a process we can call basic spirituality. Whether you are a believer or a nonbeliever, this kind of spirituality is essential. As human beings, subjected to similar conditions of life and encountering familiar adversities, we need to develop these basic spiritual values. They facilitate our daily existence and create a more pleasant environment.

Granted that these basic values should be taught and modelled at home early in life when the character of a child is being formulated, yet it is never too late, even from an adult point of view, to reconsider these values for your own self today. Being a mature adult endowed with a mental capacity, good intentions, and the desire to have a healthier and happier life, you can slowly cultivate these values one at a time and integrate them into your daily actions.

Of course, if you belong to a church, a temple, or a mosque, the task of cultivating your basic values is easier and more effective. Involvement in a religious group can create a feeling of belonging, communal ties, a caring connection with people. The dynamics of a group interacting and pursuing a common goal under the guidance of a trained spiritual leader can be most powerful.

A meaningful spiritual framework in which you share understanding of issues with others and in which you find support enables you to face life's adversities with courage and understanding. It can give you the feeling of acceptance. It can offer you opportunities to discover a sense of purpose in your personal life and help you attain a happier attitude.

The power of faith generated by a religion is interwoven into the lives of millions. Faith has sustained countless people through difficult times. Sometimes faith operates in small quiet ways, sometimes in profound transformative experiences. Occasionally, examples of the sustaining power of faith find their way onto the front pages of newspapers.

In your personal life, you must have heard or witnessed at least one example of the way in which religious faith offered concrete help to someone in time of trouble. During this writing, I have seen clear evidence of the power of faith in my own family. Sonia, my twenty-four-year-old niece, suffered from a disease known as anorexia nervosa, a pathological loss of appetite of psychological origin. Her parents took her from one specialist to another with not much success. Sonia went from 110 pounds to 52 pounds, a mere skeleton. Drugs, doctors, therapy, and hospitalization proved futile. Ignoring and refusing to accept any outside help, Sonia banked on her faith. Close relatives and friends prepared for her funeral. As a last resort, her parents joined their daughter in her belief in prayer, confident that the Healer Lord Jesus would make Sonia well. Today, Sonia has regained her health. Her attitude toward life has improved immensely, and she is planning to be engaged to Anthony, a fine young man, at Christmas time.

Sonia and her parents, because of their strong faith in an omniscient and loving God, were able to withstand intense hardship for many years. They found comfort and hope in their conviction that God would answer their prayers and ultimately reveal His love to them. Their faith was rewarded.

Although some of the rewards of faith are based on a specific experience of a particular person or family, there are other strength-giving features of a spiritual life that are available to you. Even if you are overwhelmed by life's problems, your belief can offer you hope in the face of adversity, suffering, and death.

God did not create the universe and our planet Earth as a place of perpetual happiness. God never intended life to be a continuously joyful experience designed to block out hardship and pain. Nor did God create us to be passive recipients of goods or inert social couch potatoes, oblivious to the opportunities around us. God gave each of us a certain potential and then designed us to be at our most satisfied state when we are living up to that potential.

We are created with an intense, built-in desire to live life to its fullest, to operate at peak performance. God makes Himself available, through His abiding Spirit in us, to help us achieve our potential. Intuitively, we want to be all that God created us to be. Jesus said, "I have come that they may have life, and have it to the full" (John 10:10). There is a great deal of joy in participating in life and living, using what is available to us for our well-being and for the benefit of other people. There is a lot of pain and frustration if we sit back and listen to clever advertisements and commercial appeals that promote substitutes for fulfillment.

Rodney had taken the apathy road, oblivious to where it would lead him. "I don't care!" seemed to reflect his total attitude and personal appearance. E-mail was his way of connecting with the world, and television was his refuge. He ate very little, mostly junk food; his family was little more than an annoyance. He rejected any sort of suggestion or good advice. "I don't bother anybody. Why can't you all leave me alone?" he shouted. Unable to keep a job for any length of time, he lived on money borrowed from his parents. Although he was only in his early thirties, both his work and his future were in jeopardy. He had given up on life.

Sandra, in her late twenties, was at the opposite end of the spectrum. Rodney acknowledged his hopeless perception of life; Sandra used sundry activities to hide her fears. She was always busy and tired. As she put it, "My life is an ongoing rush." She exercised regularly, and if a new vitamin appeared on the market, she was among

the first to experiment with it. She moved from relationship to rela-
tionship, staying only until the initial thrill wore off. She did not miss
an opportunity to go partying, and after the second drink her loud
voice and laughter temporarily allowed her to forget her emptiness.

When they were individually interviewed, Rodney and Sandra
claimed no religious interests of any kind. Although their parents
attended church regularly, they didn't want any part of it. Sandra,
the more outspoken of the two, said, "How can I believe in a God
who allows hatred, hunger, sickness, and war?" She was torn be-
tween her perception of God and her societal involvements. Rodney,
on the other hand, was vague about his belief in God. He said, "I
don't really know if God exists, but if He does, I don't know how to
find Him. I believe in being kind to people, treating them right, not
hurting anyone." Beneath such statements hide the human mystery,
a thirst for something that the world alone cannot give.

There are thousands of Rodneys and Sandras whose tears over a
hectic lifestyle are not visible because they are tears of an ailing soul,
crying quietly each day and seeking healing. Some men are variations
of Rodney: they haven't given up yet; they are coasting. A miracle
may occur on their way, and maybe good fortune will fall into their
lap. Some women are variations of Sandra: they are searching for the
ideal, or they are hiding in the fantasy of soap operas. Most of them
experience those moments of pain when they have to ask, "What's
wrong with me and my life?"

In his book *Care of the Soul*, Thomas Moore offers a worthwhile
answer for our consideration:

> The great malady of the twentieth century, implicated in all our
> troubles and affecting us individually and socially, is the "loss of
> soul." When soul is neglected, it doesn't just go away; it appears
> symptomatically in obsessions, addictions, violence, and loss of
> meaning. Our temptation is to isolate these symptoms or try to
> eradicate them one by one; but the root problem is that we have
> lost our wisdom about the soul, even our interest in it.

In the hubbub of daily living, many of us lose perspective. We are
not simply physical beings; we are also spiritual realities, bodies with
the indwelling spirit, our soul. Our soul is often overshadowed in
our search for joy and happiness and overlooked in the pursuit of
material possessions.

Even in vibrant middle age, men and women spend time speculating on a way to reach a place in life where they can coast, where no pain or trouble can find them. For some individuals it is called retirement. For others, it is an idealized earthly paradise of perpetual bliss. Those who never reach that goal die believing they have missed out on the secret to happiness. Some of those who do reach retirement often die of boredom and purposelessness. However, the most exciting retirees I have encountered in my life are those who define retirement as getting a new set of treads on the old tires so they can be ready for the next twenty-five thousand miles — "re-tired" and ready to go.

Most professionals in the healing arts agree that the people who are the most satisfied and fulfilled are those who can hardly wait to get up in the morning, do some gymnastics, take a shower, have breakfast, and get going to where they feel their presence and contribution at work are needed.

We may agree that a good job in which we can find fulfillment and one that provides substantial income for our needs is worthy of pursuing. To belong to a healthy family and to emerge from it every morning refreshed and revitalized is a great blessing. A warm and nurturing environment to return to in the evening after a hard day's work is soothing to the soul. These pursuits are not unattainable. They are states of mind and body that can be accomplished, not through high positions in society or the accumulation of material wealth, but through a genuine effort to accept your current reality, whatever it is, and to realize that within you lies a spiritual terrain that can yield abundant fruit.

Affluence and financial security are two alluring attractions that many people pursue but few attain. Once attained, for a while they do provide prestige, endless material possessions, and an external happiness. However, do they provide a sense of inner peace and joy?

A few years ago, on her program *20/20*, Barbara Walters asked the multimillionaire Ted Turner, "What is it like to be so wealthy and powerful?"

"It is an empty bag," Turner replied. In five words, the imagery stands out as a poignant reminder. Regardless of how much you have attained, it can never be enough. "Enough" of anything has no boundaries. It is a bottomless well. The wealthy man could not fill his bag. He was not as happy as one would have thought.

Joyful living is not a station in life; it is a condition of the heart. It does not come from living up to a societal design of expectations and degrees of performance. It is not defined by what others expect of you. It is defined by what you realistically expect of your self and of others. You cannot find inner joy by comparing your own accomplishments to what others have done or intend to do. Instead, it is found by living with the knowledge that you are operating at your own peak of performance, using gratefully the gifts, talents, and abilities that God gave you to their full intended extent. Does living with awareness that God is the Giver of all good things bring you comfort, fame, or giddy happiness? Not necessarily. But it just might bring you peace, power, and purpose.

When you find your self tempted to ask the sad question, "Is this all there is?" put your hand on your heart and hear the voice: "That's not all there is. There's more."

In spite of frustrations, disappointments, and struggles, there is much more to experience and to accomplish.

For Your Consideration

~ If you want to get the most out of life, it is essential that you first discover a purpose worth living for. With that purpose in mind, you can set goals that will consistently lead toward that end. Initially, start with short-term goals; they are easier to attain. A purpose-oriented life is a life full of exciting possibilities.

~ Much of the emptiness found in our busy lives is directly traced to a lack of purpose. Material objects can fill our houses and our garages, providing some necessary yet temporary conveniences. As much as some of these possessions entertain for a while, do they provide lasting joy?

~ In our speed-oriented world where immediate satisfaction becomes an issue, think of the potential of slowing down and enjoying life. If you maintain a hurried pace, not only will you miss the scenery by going too fast; you might even miss a sense of the direction you are going and why you are going there.

~ Develop some interest in life that gives you inner satisfaction. It may be an interest in a person or a group of people who pursue things that you may enjoy. You may start attending a church, a temple, or a mosque. Whether you are a reader or not, consider reading a book or listening to relaxing music. The world is full of possibilities, simply bursting with rich treasures that you could cherish with only a little effort on your part.

~ It is a challenge worthwhile pursuing to start looking honestly and fearlessly at who you are beneath all the surface trappings that surround you. To your surprise, you may discover that appearances, possessions, achievements, physical strength, talent, or intellect are only temporary and eventually fade away. What remains is your spiritual dimension, your eternal soul.

Chapter 18

THE TRANSFORMING POWER
OF FAITH AND PRAYER

Humans, through their faith, have magnified their strength, their courage, and their power. The greatness of mankind has been displayed by obscure individuals who have had faith in an idea or an ideal. Faith and prayer combined is a force that comforts, inspires and tides us over the difficulties of life that tend to obstruct our path to self-restoration. — THURMAN FLEET

MIDDLE-AGED DR. NORMAN claimed for many years to be an agnostic and a borderline atheist. Eloquently, he made statements such as: "God is a myth." "Religion is for the ignorant masses and naive population that need a crutch to get through the adversities of life." "Churches, temples, and mosques are power institutions that provide temporary comfort and keep people from destroying themselves."

Dr. Norman's statements might carry elements of truth if we did not observe and consider the trend of our times — the search for spirituality. We cannot ignore the fact that these masses, which resort to religious institutions, go to bookstores for spiritual reading, and attend retreats, besides finding temporary comfort, discover direction for their lives.

In 1931, Carl G. Jung stated what is applicable today: "Religions are psychotherapeutic systems in the most actual meaning of the word, and in the widest measure, and no matter what the world thinks about religious experience, the one who has it, possesses the great treasure of a thing that has provided him or her with the source of life, meaning, and beauty, and has given a new splendor to the world and to mankind."

What Dr. Norman fails to acknowledge is the intention of the believer. Who knows what yearning lies in the depth of the human heart? Who knows what miracles believers witness in their own lives?

What is also of great significance is the motivation of an individual or of a family who earnestly seek a sanctuary and receive consoling spiritual information rather than theological abstractions. Is it fear that compels them or is it faith in a God Who is the Creator of all things visible and invisible, Who is a sovereign power in charge of the universe, Who is the Father of the human race?

Faith in God is a gift. It is not merely intellectual assent to a set of dogmas. It is, rather, an attitude, a whole program for life, a renewal, an inner transformation that makes everything pass into a level of reality immensely more substantial and actual than the superficial contacts of ordinary days. Faith is offered to those who surrender with humility, seeking Him in all good will and objectivity, knocking at the door of truth, and hoping for an answer. The knocking may take a lifetime, or the door may open at the first approach. It is a challenge. Either we live by faith or we die of anguish, fear, frustration, pressure, and tension. We have a choice.

Now the question: *What is faith?*

"What is the difference between faith and knowledge?" asked a Sunday school teacher of her eighth-grade students. No one was quite sure what the difference was. Then Nancy, one of the precocious girls, volunteered the answer. "I'm the oldest of five children in our family. My mother knows that all five of us are her children. That's knowledge. My father believes that all five of us are his children. That's faith."

It was a rather humorous answer, but it pointed out that knowledge is an understanding gained through an experience. Faith, however, implies a confident belief in the truth or trustworthiness of a person, idea, or value. The definition of faith is more concise in the Epistle to the Hebrews: "Faith is the assurance of things hoped for, the conviction of things not seen."

What, then, is the meaning of faith for us? Based on the above definition we can declare that faith is an inherent attribute of the human soul. Faith must be developed in all of its phases in order to manifest its complete character, which is a transforming power. Once we attain real faith, we will be more authentically open to dancing with life in whatever form it presents itself. This kind of faith in a loving God brings great joy and engagement with life, as well as less fear, hesitation, and aversion as we think about what tomorrow will bring. It allows us to experience more awe toward the mysteries of life and more appreciation.

"How can I develop this faith?" you may ask. You develop it through awareness of who you are, namely, God's creation, and through prayer. The path, as always, begins beneath your feet with the first step you take. Where do you stand right now? This is where you begin. Let me be your companion.

Suppose you make it a reality of your life that there is a God, a powerful force that is holding all things together without your conscious control. What if you could see in your daily life the working of that force? What if you start believing that this sort of power loves you and cares for you? Such a belief would allow you the opportunity to sit back for a few minutes each day and relax.

Your physical body is at work every moment. Your heart beats, your lungs breathe, your ears hear, your eyes see, your tongue tastes, your teeth chew, your stomach digests, your body grows and changes. Here you have an array of mechanisms working all the time with a brilliance of design and efficiency no human effort could ever begin to match. You don't have to make them work; they just do, as long as you don't hinder them.

Our planet revolves around the sun, seeds become flowers, embryos become babies — all with no help from us. Their movement is built into a natural system. We are an integral part of that system. We can let our lives be guided gratefully and directed by the same wise force that makes flowers grow, or we can direct our lives ourselves.

To trust in God Who moves the universe and is in charge of our lives takes faith. Faith is not blind; it is visionary. Faith is a psychological awareness of an unfolding force for good constantly at work in all dimensions and concerned with those qualities of the human spirit — love and compassion, forgiveness, patience, tolerance, contentment, a sense of responsibility, a sense of harmony — that bring happiness to both self and others. Our attempt to direct this force only interferes with it. Our willingness to accept and relax into it allows it to work on our behalf.

Externally the universe supports our physical survival. Photosynthesis in plants and plankton in the ocean produce the oxygen we need in order to breathe. It is important to respect the laws that rule the physical universe, because violation of these laws threatens our survival. When we pollute the oceans or destroy plant life, we are destroying our support system, and so we are destroying our selves.

Internally, the equivalent of oxygen — what we need to survive emotionally and spiritually — is love, and the ramifications of love are acceptance, understanding, justice, compassion, and caring for others. Human relationships exist to produce love. When we pollute our relationships with unloving thoughts and attitudes or destroy them with betrayals, jealousies, and infidelities, we are threatening our emotional stability. As surely as a lack of oxygen will kill us, so will a lack of love. Think about it. If we don't love our selves or love someone or feel loved, we become emotionally anemic.

Every day we take care of our physical self. We eat properly, we rest, we exercise, we work, we maintain a healthy attitude, and we stay in touch with a significant other, sharing our life according to our needs. We are in charge. But the power that keeps us alive is beyond our control. Of course we can control what and how much we eat, but the power that converts our food into flesh, blood, bones, and physical strength is beyond our control. We have learned consciously or unconsciously to trust that power, just as we trust the power that holds galaxies together.

If we wish to develop a sense of spiritual life, we need to trust and surrender to God. "In God we trust" is imprinted on our currency. "Surrender" means relinquishing our attachment to results. When we surrender to God, we let go of our attachment to external happenings and become more concerned with what happens on the inside. To place something in the hands of God is to surrender it, mentally, to the protection and care of the benevolent God.

You may have noticed that when you attach your self to results — as you give advice, invest money, cultivate your garden, cook a meal, do your laundry — you find it difficult to give up control. Surely you want to see results. No one can challenge your expectations. Yet there is another reality. Can you honestly be sure of the outcome of any endeavor? Think of any experience you have had when you actually made the effort. Now translate that in a spiritual way. For example, when things are beyond your control and you may appeal to your Creator for help: "Dear God, help my child to get well." "Help my son to find direction in life." "Help me get this job." "Help me to win the lottery." "Make Mary fall in love with me." There is nothing wrong with such human wishes. But when we focus on results, expecting things to happen immediately and the way we want them, we become anxious. We might feel better by saying, "Lord, this is what I want to see happen, but I leave the results of each of my requests in Your hands. I trust that You are a loving God and

You will grant me whatever is of benefit to me. May Your will be done. Amen."

This sort of surrender to God's will is to accept the fact that God loves you and provides for you, because God loves and provides for all life abundantly. Think of the magnitude of nature — the seeds that fall on the ground, the trees, the animals that live and multiply. Think of the sun rising every morning, the rain, the snow, the changing seasons.

The whole universe is interwoven with the spirit of God. Spiritual laws exist and operate regardless of our beliefs about them. For those who apply them, they work. Would a farmer doubt that seeds, once planted, will sprout, given proper conditions? Is the farmer a simpleton for believing in that process? Why not embrace our own spiritual reality and harness it for our greatest good? Instead of resisting spiritual principles and practices, let them benefit our lives.

We wish for inner peace. We desire to attain fulfillment and joy; we need to relax and smell the flowers. We need to feel loved, and we need to keep that love always in focus in every situation. In spite of the fact that most people are always in a hurry, they take time to pause for prayer. They do so, not because they are in dire need of something urgent, but because they feel an inner yearning to talk to God, to tell God what they are unable to tell another, not even their closest of friends. For many people know that God is the closest and most intimate friend a person can have. This can be a start to our spiritual life. It can be a change; we can become more sensitive, more attractive and interesting people. It is truly a challenge.

Envision yourself at this hour holding a cup. If your cup is already full, nothing or nobody can pour more into it. If it is empty, it has room and the potential to receive. When you think that you have things already figured out, that you know it all, then you are not receptive or teachable. Insight cannot dawn on a mind that is saturated with knowledge and information. Surrendering to God is a process of emptying the mind of unnecessary clutter. "Create in me a clean heart, O God; renew a right spirit within me. Restore to me again the joy of Your salvation, and make me willing to obey You," cried David the Psalmist.

Christ's admonition, "Become as a little child," is significant. Little children do not think they know what everything means. In fact, they know that they do not know. They ask someone older and wiser to explain things to them. At times, we are like children who do not know, but we think we do.

The wise person does not pretend to know what is impossible to know. When we admit that we do not know something, it can be an empowering statement. *En eitha oti outhen eitha* (one thing I know is that I do not know), claimed Socrates.

I love the definition of a saint given by a child: It is a colorful window that the sun shines through. This is our challenge: to let the light of God, His presence, shine through us. God's light shines most brightly within us when we relax and let it be, allowing it to shine away our grandiose illusions. It is a sparkle in people that money cannot buy. It is an invisible strength with visible results.

Something amazing happens when we surrender to God. We melt into another world. It is a gentle melting into who we really are. We let down our armor, our excuses and defenses, and discover the strength of our own soul. The world changes when we change. The world softens when we soften. Some people out there may love us when we choose to be loving and caring. There is a line in a song from the play *Les Miserables* that says, "To love another person is to see the face of God."

What an accomplishment it would be if we could see other humans as God's creation to be respected. What a difference it would make in our interaction with others if we learned to acknowledge that each person possesses a spark of divinity within, a soul that never dies. In every relationship, we can teach either love or fear. To teach is to demonstrate. When we demonstrate a loving spirit toward others, we learn that we are lovable. But when we demonstrate fear or negativity, we learn self-condemnation, and we feel frightened. When we shake a finger at someone, figuratively or literally, we will not succeed in correcting that person's wrongful behavior. Treating a person with compassion and forgiveness can be much more productive. People treated with respect are likely to be less defensive and more likely to be open and to see the better part of their complex selves. Some people are not aware of their behavior. They would do things differently if they knew how. Attacking them on a point of their vulnerability pushes them deeper into the mire of despair.

As we ascend the road to spirituality, we need to be conscious of what we choose to perceive, our brother's or sister's faults or their kindness. We know that people are not perfect — including you and me. Initially it may be difficult to express externally our internal potential to do good. We know there is good in each one of us. However, when we are rude, judgmental, cruel, or intolerant of others, such negativity implies we are afraid. Fear breeds more fear, isolation, and loneliness.

Living in this world of fear teaches us to respond instinctively, and we react with anger or defensiveness. Of course there are situations that upset us; our feelings get hurt; we react angrily. At times we seek revenge. Is revenge ever a satisfactory solution? Since when did "an eye for an eye and a tooth for a tooth" make any sense? A more viable solution is proposed by Christ: "Turn the other cheek," meaning turn toward the direction of the Holy Spirit, the Comforter Who is ever present, the Giver of Life, the Treasure of all Goods. Invite Him to come into your life, to point direction, and to cleanse all your stains and heal all your wounds.

Spirituality helps us to learn to treat our selves and others with love and with the spirit of acceptance. We do not need to judge anyone; we must seek to heal and help. St. Paul introduces the idea of forbearance: "We the strong, we have an obligation to endure the wrongdoings of the weak and not try to please ourselves" by seeking to discipline or punish them. That is not our job. God balances the wrongs, not by attack, judgment, or punishment but by unconditional acceptance, forgiveness, and love. When tempted to attack someone, get even, or seek vengeance, we know a little better. Now we can try something new and different. Alcoholics Anonymous suggests the familiar axiom, "Let go and let God" — and it works.

This chapter would be incomplete if we did not explore the power of prayer, even in few paragraphs. An integral part of faith is prayer. Prayer is talking to God in a simple and personal way. We do not have to use a dictionary to discover fancy words. A simple vocabulary that comes from the heart suffices. It is through prayer that our faith is strengthened. Every religion points out the power and importance of prayer in human life. The dire need for prayer is adequately summarized by St. Francis of Assisi:

> Lord, make me an instrument of Your peace,
> where there is hatred, let me sow love;
> where there is injury, pardon;
> where there is doubt, faith;
> where there is despair, hope;
> where there is darkness, light;
> where there is sadness, joy.

> O Divine Master, grant that I may not so much seek
>   to be consoled as to console;
>   to be understood as to understand;
>   to be loved as to love.
>   For it is in giving that we receive;
>   it is in pardoning that we are pardoned;
>   and it is in dying that we are born to eternal life. Amen.

A glimpse at the world today illustrates all too clearly the importance of prayer. Tremendous upheaval, conflict, and senseless brutality are evident on many global stages. In the face of this, you may ask how prayer fits into the picture. Is it a magic wand to remove injustice and crime, to restore peace, rejuvenate the environment, feed the hungry, shelter the homeless, eliminate greed and corruption? No. It is a means toward such ends. Prayer serves as a viable tool for transformation, a vehicle to enable us to experience the spiritual fabric of our selves and of our fellow human beings. By so doing we can gradually learn to live in a manner both positive and uplifting. This rediscovery of our selves in a spiritual context may truly be the only way we can — as a world, country, society, family, and individual — survive and thrive.

Prayer is the unique channel of relating with God. Our soul yearns for a relationship with God, which can be attained only through constant prayer. Regular prayer serves to remind us that we belong to God, and without His presence, our life is empty and without direction. God reveals His will to our minds. He opens the way for us to follow. He removes the obstacles. As we acknowledge our faults and shortcomings, we experience the satisfaction of His forgiveness. He is a God of unconditional love, compassion, and mercy. "Trust in the Lord with all your heart and do not lean on your own understanding. In all your ways acknowledge Him, and He will make your paths straight" (Prov. 3:5–6).

Through the practice of prayer we find comfort and joy in God's presence. In the process of restoring our self, we begin to see the light of our spiritual self. Then our heart takes over to speak the language of the soul. We praise God through our feelings of gratitude; we worship Him and ask for help and guidance through a receptive ear: "Ask, and it will be given to you; seek, and you will find; knock, and it will be opened to you. For everyone who asks receives, and to him who knocks it will be opened" (Matt. 7:7–8).

The true meaning of prayer was clarified by Christ when His disciples came to Him and said, "Lord teach us to pray." He replied, "When you pray, do not heap up empty phrases... pray in this way," and He gave them the ultimate form of prayer, universally known as the Lord's Prayer. A brief interpretation of this prayer may help to make it a personal spiritual property for you that can give a new dimension to your life.

Our Father in heaven:

I am now aware of the infinite and eternal Presence of God in whom I live, and by whose power I think, feel, and create.

Hallowed be Your Name:

Your Presence within me is whole and complete. It is the Spirit that heals, the force that inspires acceptance, love, caring for others, the force that harmonizes life.

Your Kingdom come, Your will be done on earth as it is in heaven:

I am God's choice to be His co-worker in His creation. I now let His plan for me unfold in me and through me, to be trusted to my care. My desire for betterment is God's desire to fulfill that which He is expressing as me; I surrender to His way. I see my self doing that which God sees me as being.

Give us this day our daily bread:

It is not just bread that I need; I need God's grace to sustain my soul. I cannot be separated from the Giver of Life. He is the Treasurer of all Blessings. I am one of the heirs of His spiritual treasures. I will daily remind my self that I am His child.

Forgive us our debts as we forgive our debtors:

God's Presence in me is my potential for dissolving all conflicts and transgressions. The Presence is Love, and it is Love in me and through me as I forgive. It releases me as I loosen and let go of all my limited thoughts about my self and others.

And lead us not into temptation, but deliver us from evil:

God's Presence in me is my light and my salvation. There is no darkness in the light, and there can be no darkness in me when

I am established in a spiritual unity with the Presence of God within me — which is better than light and safer than any other familiar way.

For Yours is the Kingdom and the power and the glory for ever. Amen.

In all that I seek in my life to be or to do or to have, I humbly realize that in the Presence of God I feel empowered to think my every thought and aspiration. God empowers my will to commence a desired project. God provides my strength to endure, my power to achieve noble goals and to cherish the glory of all my accomplishments. This is the Truth, and it is now done. Thank you, Lord. Amen.

For Your Consideration

~ Faith and prayer can be the keynote of your success, faith that you are of divine origin, that you are created by God, and that you are here for a purpose. Your inner self, the spirit within, is your guardian and trusted friend. As you pray, listen to this unseen part of you and live each day meaningfully.

~ When you transcend the limits of your being and reach out toward others whom you understand and believe in, creatively incorporating and blending your life with theirs and praying for them, then your life becomes spiritually transformed, empowered, and enriched.

~ Your prayer and inner longing to believe in God and His benevolent presence in your life will restore in you a joyful spirit, lasting harmony, and understanding, peace, and happiness. Those who lack faith in God and do not pray also lose faith in their own selves. As a result they feel unprotected and in danger, like a boat without a rudder, tossed about on the waves of life.

~ When faith takes root, it needs to be nurtured by constant prayer. When faith begins to develop in your heart, all mental clouds evaporate. As prayer lifts you to a sublime level of being, closer to your Creator, your faith overflows and touches others in a special way. You, too, will experience a great feeling of lightness in the heart.

~ If Saul of Tarsus, a blasphemer against God, could become St. Paul, a great Apostle of the Christian Gospel, then you also — regardless of who you are at this point in your life — can transform your life. You have the power and the capacity to change, provided you decide to do it. The strength to make such a decision comes from within as you pray.

Chapter 19

THE UNCOMPROMISING CHOICE

I know what you are doing. You are not cold or hot. I wish you were one or the other. But because you are lukewarm, and not hot or cold, I will spit you out of My mouth.

— Revelation 3:15–16

NOWHERE ELSE in the Bible do we find such a strong emotion ascribed to the Lord. The author addresses these words to the Laodiceans. Laodicea, a city in Asia Minor, was especially famous for its wealth. It was a great commercial and financial center, the home of millionaires. But the Laodiceans, "people of justice," as the Greek word implies, were unbearably conceited. They imagined that their wealth was a sign of God's special favor. They boasted of their spiritual riches: "Rich am I — in spiritual goods — and all along I have been getting richer and richer, and whatever I have gained I still possess, and not one single need have I" (Rev. 3:17).

It is easy to see why the author of the Book of Revelation expected to be treated by his listeners with a glow of warm affection. Instead, he found nothing but indifference. "I wish you were one or the other, hot or cold." Anything is better than indifference.

One can understand why he would have preferred the Laodiceans to be hot. But why would he have accepted a state of utter coldness? Sad as it may be, coldness is at least *honest*. We find no disguise, no concealment, no pretense. We might prefer such a state to that of insincerity or indifference. Sometimes we can expect an attitude of coldness, but we do not have to take it personally. We do not have to like it. If a person is cold or indifferent, that may be his or her nature. It is not our job to change it. We can accept it as a position that someone has chosen. But when people are false to their engagements and make promises they never fulfill, there is nothing in them we can respect. Such people cannot apply truth to themselves. They are not *real*.

"And because you are lukewarm, and not hot or cold, I will spit you out of My mouth." This image is intense. It denotes disgust and loathing at the indifference toward others that prevailed among the Laodiceans. Lukewarm, tepid, flabby, halfhearted, limp, always ready to compromise or to flatter, indifferent. "We're all good people here in Laodicea" is their attitude.

Of course you are acquainted with this attitude. Can you stand it? Can you hold a decent dialogue with someone who is lukewarm? How familiar we all are with effusive welcomes and false amenities we exchange in our everyday life with lukewarm people.

"Oh, hi! How are you?"

"I'm fine, thanks. And you?"

"Good."

"That's good."

"Yes."

"How's the family? Good?"

"Great."

"Good."

"Have a nice day."

And off goes the acquaintance. You know perfectly well that the person isn't in the least interested in you or your life.

Can you make this person your friend or your mate? Can you travel with such a person? Or can you engage him or her in a business venture?

What if this person happens to be you? Lukewarm, neither firmly positive nor firmly negative, but a wishy-washy uninterested person. Can you stand yourself? Can you feel comfortable?

A story is told of Alexander the Great. During a battle, he found a soldier hiding in the hollow of a tree.

"What is your name?" demanded Alexander.

The trembling soldier replied, "A-a-ale-le-lex-x-ander."

Alexander the Great responded, "Either change your name or your attitude."

No one else but you can change your attitude. Why change it in the first place? Either because it is offensive or because you don't like it. How are you going to free your self from that lukewarm attitude that is making trouble for you? Willpower? Discipline? Neither of these alone will free you from such an unproductive attitude unless there is an inner desire to change. Getting rid of something we dislike about our self is quite different from giving up something we like.

When the official statement was made that cigarettes were definitely dangerous to health, the sales dropped sharply because many people stopped smoking. Most who quit smoking suffered great discomfort. Most of them had no desire to give up the habit, and their minds were filled with longing to return to their old friend, the cigarette. The more they fought against the desire, the more conscious of the desire they became, until it overwhelmed them and they began to smoke again. Others who struggled against the inner pull to smoke ditched the bad companion and were happy to see the last of it. They were able to give up cigarettes. It was their decision to abandon an old and destructive habit.

Before accepting treatment to get well, alcoholics have to be thoroughly disenchanted with alcohol and what it does to them. They have to know that there is no way they can drink even a small amount of alcohol. They must know every aspect of the enemy. They have to see the whole wasteland alcohol makes of a life. They have to see it so clearly that they recognize they are not giving up a comforting friend. On the contrary, they are getting rid of a curse.

Who can stop us from being destructive? At times, we cannot see ourselves as we really are because we are too accustomed, too comfortable with what we do or what we say. We cannot be free until we practice the art of benevolent detachment. Developing autonomy implies hard work; having to choose to be hot or cold, active or passive, creative or destructive, is developing self. Once we decide which course to take, we have freedom, personal satisfaction, fulfillment.

When times are tough, it is beneficial to assume that, occasionally, adversity is a test of character. When work is unrewarding or money is tight and life is a matter of holding on for better days, it seems that finding relief through moral compromise might be enticing. Instead of giving in to destructive choices, say to yourself, "I'll accept my present situation until I'm ready for a change." When you are insecure, frequently you will stay with what is safe and familiar rather than take the chance of stepping out and perhaps failing. Doubt and fear can prevent you from reaching your potential. Strive to understand the feelings, and then make choices that will bring positive change to your life.

Suppose the sphere turns around and you begin to sense that prosperity is becoming your reality — a new job, a new relationship, new environment, more money. Success can be scary. Your spirit soars high, your salary increases, and so do your perks, privacy, and temptations. This is another test of character. As you look around, not everyone seems to smile at your newfound happiness. You may face jealousy or fierce competition. The security you hoped to gain by making it to the top fades. Remember that your character is not only tested with the reality of life; it is also sharpened. You can strive for balance.

Because of constant change and feelings of being *off balance,* it is essential to develop healthy coping skills. We will never catch up and be on top of all things. Accept this as all right. Put a high priority on investing time to cultivate and refine your character.

Take inventory of how you feel about your self. Is it the real you, the integral you, or is it a distorted image given to you by others? Do you see your self as a hopeless creature that nobody loves? Where did this idea come from? Do you want to change a part of this self?

Why not see your self a creature of God with a destiny to fulfill? There is no reason not to fulfill it. You cannot use your weaknesses as excuses. Instead of listening to others, why not hear God's voice through one of His prophets, Jeremiah: "For I know the thoughts and plans that I have for you, thoughts and plans for welfare and peace and not for evil, to give you hope in your final outcome" (Jer. 29:11).

Emerging technologies saturate us with the voices of humankind — both alien and harmonious — leaving little room for God's message. As we absorb their rhymes and reasons, they become part of us and we of them. They may leave us feeling either detached from the inner self or feeling indifferent toward life. Social saturation furnishes us with a multiplicity of incoherent and unrelated languages of the self. For everything we know to be true about our selves, we hear voices within that cause us to doubt and even deride our selves.

A saturated self can hardly make sense about life and living. It has a hard time making honest and pleasant contact with another human being. Relationships pull us in many directions, inviting us to play such a variety of roles that we lose the very concept of an *authentic self.* Like a kaleidoscope, with each turn our image changes. If we take our cues from the secular world, the rich and famous whose images flicker on our television screens, then it is difficult to discern the real self within each of us. Virtue and integrity are godly qualities. If we want to make them ours, we may have to let go of the desire for popularity.

Each of us is a mysterious composite of our influences and personal experiences. We are something like a computer. Millions of messages have been fed into and recorded in our brain and nervous system. Every muscle, fiber, and brain cell of our being stores these countless messages. To complicate things further, we have an *unconscious mind,* a storehouse of unacknowledged data by which we are constantly being influenced. In comparison to a most sophisticated computer, our minds are far more intricate and complicated. Simply, be true to your self. Either be hot or cold, but avoid being lukewarm.

Of course we never totally understand anyone, our selves included. But we can gain a real sense of what it is like to be the *other.* We can understand something of the inner consistency of the thoughts, feelings, and actions of another human being.

We have to learn a new way to observe our selves: nonjudgmentally. We must recognize the "what is" of our behavior. As psychiatrist Alfred Adler (1870–1937) said: "If you want to understand yourself and another person, close your ears to anything that is said or that you think, and watch only movement. What a person does is the real understanding and intention."

Develop in yourself the practice of total nonjudgmental awareness of everything you are doing. If you are against smoking but find yourself with a cigarette in your hand, sit passively by and watch yourself light it, cough, put out the match, drop ashes on yourself — observe every move you make. At the same time listen to your self saying: "I ought to give up smoking for my health's sake. What a weak character I am, smoking in spite of my decision to quit."

If you do this for a period of time, you will become aware of a curious change. It is almost as if you sat in a room where two television sets were presenting two different programs at the same time, using the same cast of characters in each one. It might seem like an old Western movie with good guys and bad guys fighting it out. You will observe that you habitually pit your two selves against each other: the ideal self versus the quality of your everyday behavior.

This process enables us to bring unconscious habits into the spotlight of total awareness. A blurred self-image about who we are and how we behave occurs in those areas where the unconscious habit is leading us astray. We cannot escape the unconscious habit while it remains at that level of nonawareness. It behaves as if it were a compulsion to drink, smoke, steal, lie, eat, or even kill.

Frank, a proud middle-aged father, had managed to stay dry for ninety days. He believed that alcohol was no longer a problem. His wife and three children were somewhat apprehensive because he had been an alcoholic for more than ten years. He reassured them that he had reformed, and although he passed the tavern every day, he was not tempted to go in. However, one day as he passed the tavern, he said to himself, "You are a strong man. You have beaten your problem. Patience and persistence made you a winner. You can have just one drink." Frank started drinking again.

Mystified and baffled, we wonder what the blind power is that drives us toward destructive behaviors quite against our conscious will. It is most important for us to know the meaning of unconscious mechanisms and the role they play in creating in us the feeling of indecision or indifference. We are talking about the unconscious habits that bait us to remain immobile or ambivalent. They are the influences from within that we ignore or keep hidden from our awareness.

Have you ever been aware of trying to make a good impression? Have you ever been aware of trying to gain personal recognition? Have you ever been aware of trying to compare your self with others around you? These actions are not necessarily preplanned. They are unconscious, emerging from a clouded self and keeping us in a state of insecurity, indecision, or passivity. They can continue to trip us up for as long as we remain unaware that such activity is our own choice and leads to self-defeat.

One might say: "As long as I can make a good impression upon others, as long as I can gain recognition, as long as I compare my self with others, I justify my existence or I feel good." Could that be what you want out of life? When you gradually see with total awareness that such behavior leads to your own emotional deterioration, you will choose to get rid of it as soon as possible.

"Vigilance" is a good word to remember. The only way to have an exciting and a joyful life is to be vigilant of your thoughts, feelings, and actions. You are no longer bound to your past. Regrets, recriminations, and alibis based on your past experiences are no longer significant. You have nothing to hide or defend. When you deal with the here-and-now concept, your present life, your mind is free from your yesterdays. You are responsible only for this moment of your existence. As you confront circumstances from moment to moment, you have a choice: you can be either hot or cold. It is a waste of labor to be lukewarm.

Lukewarm individuals are aliens separated from their native land, without rights of citizenship. Individuals who reject the *now* alien-

ate their native inherent abilities and flee to another country, one of
wishes, dreams, and ideals. Life is being, and *all being is now*. Life can
be neither postponed nor transposed. Alienation from reality, in its
extreme, is psychosis — a flight from reality into dreams and fantasy.

Physical and emotional well-being is possible only as long as we
are firmly planted in the present. The problems of life demand re-
sponse and activity. Any evasion of *now* is a way of trying to postpone
activity.

If we settle for a mediocre self, if we accept a lukewarm attitude
toward life, we become passive-receptive victims of oncoming circum-
stances. The effort to escape the now by a flight into fantasy is not hot
and not cold but lukewarm; it can be called living on the deferred-
payment plan — that is, promising our selves rewards tomorrow. We
say to our selves: "I'll make a decision tomorrow. I'll take action
tomorrow." In order to live tomorrow, we do not live today. This
is a world of the eternal now, however; there is no tomorrow. Who
guarantees our presence here in the tomorrow?

We must consciously choose between two ways of facing life:
Either we live in direct spontaneous contact with the emerging now
and respond to life with a sense of responsibility and gratitude for
what is, or we live fearfully on the deferred-payment plan as an alien
from reality in a world of inertia and wishful thinking. Here our chal-
lenge becomes evident: either we believe in a loving God the Creator,
Provider, and Sustainer of Life Who cares for His creation, or we do
not. There is no middle road; there are no shades of gray. We strive
to be hot or cold, but not lukewarm. The choice is uncompromising.

For Your Consideration

~ A fundamental fact about life is that we have *choices*. Having
to choose implies that a selection must be made among various
possibilities. To choose implies to prefer. To prefer some one
thing, one action, one style, one way, necessarily demands the
discarding or eliminating of other options.

~ Making a choice and leaving behind us other possibilities is hard
because we like to hold on to things that are familiar, although
not necessarily beneficial.

~ Begin with choices about matters of little or no importance in
themselves. For example, take one street in preference to an-

other, or when in a restaurant, choose a meal different from the one you usually have. This will heighten your awareness of your ability to make choices.

~ In the process of restoring your self, remember that a basic choice is the *choice between past and present.* Old ways of functioning may no longer be productive for you. Do you want to hold on to them?

~ Like an artist, take time to put the final touches upon your self. Once you have discovered ways that work for you, throw your self boldly and joyfully into the adventure of self-restoration and invite God into your life to provide sustenance and direction.

Chapter 20

BECOMING SPIRITUAL

O Lord and Master of my life,
   Take away from me the will to be lazy and sad;
   The desire to get ahead of other people and to boast and brag.

Give me instead a pure heart and humble spirit,
   The will to be patient with other people and to love them.
O Lord and King, let me realize my own mistakes
   And keep me from judging what other people do.
For You are blessed now and forever. Amen.

— St. Ephraim of Syria

WE ARE BORN into a physical world, surrounded and raised by physical people, nurtured with food in a material environment. From an early age, we sense our physical needs and become aware of our bodies. We see our bodies growing and becoming stronger. In the process, the growing person experiences needs — physical, emotional, and spiritual. As we meet these needs through harmonization of all parts of our personality — good and bad, ugly and beautiful — we form and conform to our self-image.

Our willingness to perceive our selves and the universe around us as God's creation is the first step we take in faith. And in the unfolding workings of faith, our spiritual life begins. As we grow, most of us realize that beyond our physical self there is something within our personhood that keeps us alive and makes us conscious of who we are.

What is this something? It is the invisible part of self, and once it leaves the body, we stop breathing — we die. Our physical self, although intact and perhaps deformed in some way, either because of age or because of illness, is no longer functional. Something departs from the once-upon-a-time beautiful body, leaving it lifeless. What is this part that keeps the body alive? Most religions call it the soul, the psyche; others call it the spirit — *pneuma*. What you call it is of no importance. It may not be easy for you to accept the idea that as well as having a visible body, you also are invisible. You may think that only the visible world has reality and structure. It may be hard for you to conceive the possibility that our inner world — which we know as thought, justice, love, truth, feeling, and imagination — may have a real structure and exist in its own space, although untouchable by our physical senses. Your invisible self, the part of you that is not your physical sensory self, is the area that we will explore now. We will call it "spirit." The Greek word is *pneuma,* which comes from the word *pnoe,* meaning "breath."

In the beginning, when God created the universe, over the abyss roamed the Spirit of God, a creative force giving form and shape to the creation. According to the Book of Genesis, when the Creator of the Universe created Adam, the first human being, He breathed upon him and gave him life. It is this divine breath that keeps us alive and harmonizes our development.

Once we accept God as the Creator, implicitly we arrive at the notion that the whole of creation is a by-product of His love. Love creates. And that which is created by love is cared for lovingly. If we humans believe that there is a Creator who cares, sustains, and maintains the universe, then we are assured that His life-giving breath is available to us each moment we are alive.

It is inevitable that many who explore the misty country of the soul will indulge in doubts or disbelief, but an honest research into the nature of a human being will discover the presence of the life-giving breath, the soul. If we could possibly conceive of the workings of the subconscious mind — where buried memories, buried guilts, and buried impulses germinate for years and then break out into strange flowerings — then the pursuit of the soul would not be such an arduous task and would be a more rewarding effort. It could provide the meeting-ground for God and the human being.

From the perspective of the present moment, if you were to take a mental journey into the past and studiously look at every stage of your development, you would become aware of some kind of invisible dynamic holding together all the experiences of your life. These experiences — good, bad, horrible, or sublime — like small precious stones, form a mosaic, a unique image. It is your spiritual self that tells you: This is you.

Such a discovery would strike a chord of hope about your inner nature that has been silenced in an age of high technology and scientific achievements. This awareness would trigger in you a new vision, a triumph over flesh and blood. Scientists of our times should seek to anchor their spirit on God instead of attributing their success to a superior intellect or to chance and randomness. The more you deal with science, the harder it is to understand the universe without God.

Two thousand years ago, St. Paul spoke to the skeptical Athenians, saying: "In Him we live and move and have our being." This statement may be reassuring to members of the scientific society who progressively realize that beyond the physical world something exists in all life that defies logic.

As you hear these lines, make a move beyond logic and rational thinking and tune in to your inner self. For a few precious moments stay in touch with your invisible self to see if you can influence your physical reality.

Throughout history, major personalities who shaped the church through their exemplary lives taught us about the incredible power that resides within each individual, the power of love with its multi-dimensional benefits. It seems ironic the way this power is used in our times. Nowadays, people in powerful positions seek more power. One way to attain more power is to overpower and control other people. And since there is no such thing as enough power, leaders of nations build more and more powerful weapons, declare wars, invade other countries, kill innocent populations.

The proliferation of guns among the younger generation is another sad reality of our day. It is beyond our comprehension how anyone can have so little respect for the life of another that he considers killing is a matter of little consequence. Crime and violence have reached epidemic proportions and now provide evening entertainment for television viewers. Although adults are able to distinguish good from evil, young viewers are programmed to think that what they see is the normal way of life.

As we become aware of the degree of evil that exists in our world, we can make an effort to combat it by doing what is good and beneficial to the spirit. Simply put, we must become spiritual people.

A practical way to get started is to explore the following statements and redefine what it means to you to be a spiritual person.

1. By design, you are a spiritual person. Say to your self: "I am both body and spirit, visible and invisible." And while you are still possessing a body, allow your self to experience the yearnings of

your soul. For example: Contemplate the concept of love with its many ramifications. Contemplate loving — loving someone and being loved. Contemplate the idea of caring for others. Express admiration for the wonders of nature. Take a blade of grass in your fingers and ask: Who tells you to grow?

2. A spiritual person is never alone. Teachers, mentors, spiritual guides, books, and tools that elevate the spirit and enhance our being are available. Seek them at your church or temple or your local library. See the world around you as a laboratory for growth and learning. Get deeper into your self and learn. Besides your parents that caused your birth, a Supreme Being gave you the gift of life. God, this Supreme Being, not only gave you life but continues to sustain your life. You are never alone; you can appeal to God for guidance.

3. A spiritual person recognizes that there are external powers: government, military and police forces, financial firms, health organizations, insurance companies. Regardless of how strong external power is, it can control our external existence only. It has no power over the soul, because the inner part of our person-hood is empowered by God, the Giver of Life. Empowerment is the joy of knowing that in order to be in harmony with your self, external force is not necessary. When you abandon your need for external approval and power and align your self with your soul's purpose, you will discover the joy of loving and caring for others. It is your soul's purpose to love God. Remain connected with God that you may have abundant life.

4. A spiritual person has a sense of belonging to God's family. We are all connected, and our lives influence others and are influenced by others. If we see others as God's children and treat them as such, we eliminate conflicts, judgments, and negative thinking. Accepting others as they are, we reserve energy that we can use to cultivate our soul. That means spiritually we are able to see that the same invisible force that flows through us flows through others. They, too, have a soul, and as we treat them with care, we nurture their soul.

5. A spiritual person believes that God is present. Through the eyes of faith, try to see God present, His almighty power working in the universe. The grandeur and accuracy of the visible universe

cannot be understood without the presence of His infinite wisdom and power. From the day you become aware of your self until the end of your life, maintain awareness of His presence in your life. He is more present to you than the sunrise to the morning, than the sun to the light, than the water to the ocean, than the sap to the tree, than thought to the mind, than love to the heart. Every day remind your self of these images. With God's presence in your life, you can find joy, harmony, and peace. We are created after His image and likeness. Regardless of what is happening around us, within us we have His spirit, our soul, to guide and protect us.

6. Spiritual people are eager to cultivate their garden, the inner self, the soul. A spiritual person is after the fruit of the spirit, which consists of love, joy, peace, compassion, goodness, kindness, faith, humility, and discipline. These ingredients are imperative for our success. For the spiritual person, success is achieved by pursuing the fruit of the spirit in all its dimensions. Living a purposeful life, loving, caring, and serving others may be a slow process. But the concept, that we have been created to love and to be loved, eases our journey and brings us great reward.

7. A spiritual person knows about the amazing power of prayer. The moment we think of prayer, there is an instant tuning-in with the Almighty. Some of us turn to prayer only in time of trouble, and some of us are faithful about saying our prayers, but strange to say, very few of us know how to pray. One of the greatest joys of becoming a spiritual person is learning to pray, to connect with the ultimate power, our Creator. Actually, once you know how to pray, you will feel lighter, more joyful, more creative and productive than you ever felt before. After your prayerful moment, you will walk out into the world stronger, with a secret power in your soul.

8. A spiritual person hears the inner voice — call it intuition if you like. But intuition is much more than a thought about something. It is as if you receive a gentle prod to behave in a certain way or to avoid something that might be dangerous or unhealthy. These inner intuitive expressions are almost like having a dialogue with God. Pay attention to your intuition, that strong feeling of something, that sixth sense suggesting a particular ac-

tion or behavior; follow such inner inclinations. Intuition may guide you in a direction of growth and purpose. If you ignore it, you will never know the meaning of it.

9. Spiritual people do not align their active selves with the tools of power in a war against evil. They maintain what they believe to be good and beneficial to the other. They waste no energy talking against the wrongs of our society; they model what is good. They do not claim that philanthropic institutions must feed the hungry; instead, they make sandwiches or prepare meals for the hungry. Although war makes spiritual people angry and frustrated, they do not rebel against it; rather, they use their energy working for peace and finding paths for reconciliation. Spiritual people do not antagonize those lured by corrupt entertainment; rather, they help young people to know the power of their minds and bodies, which are temples of the spirit. They provide a healthy environment, sound education, and activities that nourish the spirit of the young.

10. A spiritual person respects the life and essence of other people and feels a sense of responsibility toward society. Spiritual people unite their thoughts and actions to protect their environment. The earth is the Lord's, and we must treat it with reverence so that the coming generations may enjoy its fruits.

11. Spiritual people have no room in their hearts for hatred, hostility, or revenge. They have no time to invest in thinking up methods of punishment for a wrongdoer or ways of getting even. Forgiveness is their forte. They do not hold grudges; they let go of resentment. Forgiveness is an act of the heart, a virtue that most major religions teach. If we allow our inner spirit to be inundated with bitterness and revenge toward others, we will have no room for peace of mind, for harmony and love.

12. A spiritual person develops slowly, requires no long-term training, no money. As you are listening to these statements, you have already started on your spiritual journey. Now it is your choice to become a spiritual being without any obligation to join or adopt a specific religion. Simply decide that this is the way you would like to live out the remainder of your life. To attain physical fitness, you exercise according to your age and ability. Your spiritual fitness also requires close attention. Think

about the state of life in which you find your self today; consider the model we have talked about here, and then resolve to attain your spiritual fitness.

For Your Consideration

~ Each day, take a few minutes to nurture your soul. Learn to get in touch with your inner self, and know that everything in life has a purpose.

~ Try to acquire the habit of checking your self during the day and before you go to sleep. Ask your self: "How am I feeling? What am I thinking about? What am I doing?"

~ Make a list of your needs. Make sure that these are real needs and not merely wants. All we need is guidance. Ask God for it.

~ Pray for understanding and patience. Make sure you are not making unreasonable demands of your self and of God.

~ Pray with love and humility. Our Lord is a God of love. Once you engage in prayer, you will begin to feel His love, a life force and vitality within you.

EPILOGUE

IN BRINGING THIS BOOK to an end I feel excited that it will allow me to travel with you. Now that we have moved through the chapters together, I am grateful that you invited me to be a companion on your journey of self-restoration. I hope that you have enjoyed the experience. Remember: books, doctors, psychologists, wise teachers, therapists, healers, sages, philosophers, and theologians — individually or together — can help you only if you are willing to receive their help.

I trust that each of the five parts of this book has given you food for thought, ideas, and pointers toward a new direction. Perhaps you have underlined certain paragraphs that had special meaning for you. Reread these statements and incorporate them into your life, making them your own property. At this precious moment, as you are still carrying this book, imagine that you are holding my hand and we are continuing our journey together. I realize that it is time for us to separate physically from each other, but we do not have to part spiritually. We can still be connected through this writing and our faith in God. Now it is time to move on and enjoy this endowment, God's unconditional love and our faith in Him that make the power of restoration so enduring.

Because of our commitment to self-restoration, something good is going to happen. Start believing that your life is getting healthier and happier. For our human condition, this is by far the best remedy. We are now companions in the quest for healing, wholeness, and joy. By exerting our own individual will, mobilizing our own resources, neither blaming anyone for our failings nor accepting blame for the failings of others, we are taking charge of our lives. The plan for our self-restoration has begun.

BIBLIOGRAPHY

Beecher, Marguerite and Willard. *Beyond Success and Failure*. New York: Pocket Books, 1966.

Benson, Herbert, M.D. *Timeless Healing*. New York: A Fireside Book, 1996.

De Vinck, Jose. *The Yes Book*. Allendale, N.J.: Alleluia Press, 1982.

Dyer, Wayne W. *Your Sacred Self*. New York: Harper Paperbacks, 1995.

Feet, Thurman. *Rays of the Dawn*. San Antonio, Tex.: Concept-Therapy, 1976.

Flanigan, Beverly. *Forgiving the Unforgivable*. New York: Macmillan, 1998.

Gilligan, Carol. *In a Different Voice*. Cambridge, Mass.: Harvard University Press, 1982.

Kalellis, Peter M. *Pick Up Your Couch and Walk: How to Take Back Control of Your Life*. New York: Crossroad, 1998.

———. *Restoring Relationships: Five Things to Try Before You Say Goodbye*. New York: Crossroad, 2001.

McCullough, Michael E., Steven J. Sandage, and Everett L. Worthington. *To Forgive Is Human: How to Put Your Past in the Past*. Downers Grove, Ill.: InterVarsity Press, 1997.

McMahon, James M. *The Price of Wisdom*. New York: Crossroad, 1996.

Moore, Thomas. *Care of the Soul*. New York: HarperCollins, 1992.

Myss, Caroline. *Why People Don't Heal and How They Can*. New York: Three Rivers Press, 1997.

Nouwen, Henri J. M. *Here and Now*. New York: Crossroad, 1995.

Padovani, Martin H. *Healing Wounded Emotions*. Mystic, Conn.: Twenty-Third Publications, 1991.

Tickle, Phyllis A. *Rediscovering the Sacred: Spirituality in America*. New York: Crossroad, 1995.

Wimala, Bhante Y. *Lessons of the Lotus*. New York: Bantam Books, 1997.

Peter D'Arcy

THE GIFT OF THE RED BIRD
A Spiritual Encounter

"To say that *The Gift of the Red Bird* moved me deeply seems inadequate. I wept for its beauty, pain, and joy. It is a powerful testimony to how the Divine woos the soul into a sacred embrace. Paula D'Arcy's vulnerability and courage in narrating her true story of this divine encounter are remarkable."
— Joyce Rupp

"It is all a matter of seeing, but we need seers to show us how. Paula D'Arcy shatters our poor sight and shows us light."   — Richard Rohr

When Paula D'Arcy lost her husband and baby in a car crash, she began an inner search for a faith that was stronger than fear. In *Gift of the Red Bird* she shares her remarkable spiritual adventure: Paula literally journeyed alone into the wilderness for three days, allowing the Creator to speak through that creation. As she surrendered to the power of God alone, a red bird appeared and, without words, began to teach. . . .

0-8245-1956-6; $14.95 paperback

Nancy Bruning

RHYTHMS AND CYCLES
Sacred Patterns

"Nancy Bruning's wonderful walk through world culture gives a clear and comprehensive incentive to try to get our rhythm back!"
— Rev. Robert Cormier, author of *A Faith That Makes Sense*

"Wonderful! This is a deeply wise book. Nancy Bruning has a gift for exploring the neglected niches in life where the sweetness lies — finding value in every moment, every experience, even those we commonly reject."
— Larry Dossey, M.D., author of *Healing Words*

0-8245-1962-0; $19.95 paperback

crossroad

AGAINST AN INFINITE HORIZON
The Finger of God in Our Everyday Lives

"Ronald Rolheiser has mastered the old, old art of parable." — Morris West

In this prequel to the bestselling *The Holy Longing,* Rolheiser provides further insight into community, social justice, sexuality, mortality, and rediscovering the deep beauty and poetry of Christian spirituality.

0-8245-1965-5; $16.95 paperback

THE SHATTERED LANTERN
Rediscovering a Felt Presence of God

"Whenever I see Ron Rolheiser's name on a book, I know that it will be an amazing combination of true orthodoxy and revolutionary insight — and written in a clear and readable style. He knows the spiritual terrain like few others, and you will be profoundly illuminated by this lantern. Read and be astonished."
— Richard Rohr, O.F.M., Center for Action
and Contemplation, Albuquerque, New Mexico

Rolheiser teaches us that the way back to a lively faith "is not a question of finding the right answers, but of living a certain way. The existence of God, like the air we breathe, need not be proven." This work shines new light on the contemplative path of Western Christianity and offers a dynamic way forward.

0-8245-1884-5; $14.95 paperback

crossroad